MUD FLOWER

MUD FLOWER

*Surviving Schizophrenia and
Suicide Through Art*

Meghan J.M. Caughey

LUMINARE PRESS
WWW.LUMINAREPRESS.COM

Luminare Press
442 Charnelton St.
Eugene, OR 97401
www.luminarepress.com

LCCN: 2021902930
ISBN: 978-1-64388-639-8

*This book is for every person who has struggled
between the choices of life and death,
for the people who love and care about them,
and to the persons who dedicate their
lives to helping us heal.*

First Words

This book includes stories about suicide that could be potentially triggering to some people who are struggling.

It is our goal to encourage people to get the help and hope necessary to choose life instead of suicide.

If you are struggling, please reach out for help.

One excellent possible option is the National Suicide Prevention Lifeline.

Call 1-800-273-TALK (1-800-273-8255) until July 2022.

After July 2022, please call the new, easier number: 988.

The volunteers on this Lifeline are very kind and will be able to help guide you to resources to steer you through your hard time.

"Art is the highest form of hope."

G. RICHTER

ONE

I found myself wandering from room to room,
it was not yet dawn, even the birds were not
yet awake, everything was so quiet; old houses'
have their ghosts, yet the ghosts were still asleep,
so I just wandered from room to room,
alone—how long is life?

Portland, Oregon, 2018

Today the news came that I won the suicide essay contest. Shouldn't I be thrilled?

Actually, I nearly won—I got second place, so I sort of won, but not entirely.

So, I'm sort of thrilled. But not entirely.

The Organization to End Suicide sponsored the contest, which was supposed to give us, the survivors of our suicidal acts, a way to tell our stories and inspire others who are struggling with similar feelings.

When I submitted my essay, I worried that if I won, I would suddenly have the tall responsibility of representing hope to all the suicidal people in the world—the lost ones who are looking for some tiny morsel of light, who feel like they just can't take it anymore.

But I didn't win first place.

So, am I released from the responsibility of being the Messenger of Hope?

The Messenger of Hope? Oh, girl, there you go being grandiose again! You're surely no messenger of hope. Watch out!!!
Oh, hypocrite! Liar, liar!

And then, on top of everything, today was Valentine's Day.

I am struggling to not feel sorry for myself since the only Valentine I received was a text message from Kent, saying he sends his love. Usually, he sends roses and the fragrant white lilies I adore and writes about how I am so important to him. Not this year—he is newly in love with the Montessori schoolteacher. I am happy for him—shouldn't I be? I must let go of the small but nagging desire we might ever find a way to be together again. And since it probably isn't even possible for him to be monogamous and since he might move to Canada, why don't I just let go? "Just let go"? Who can ever really "just let go"? People recommend it all the time. We might try, but do we ever succeed? Sometimes I can get an elusive, little flash of how it might feel. I get a tiny little nip—a quick rush of "*aaaahhhhh.*" But it only lasts a moment. Tonight, it is impossible. Tonight, as I contemplate going to bed, most things feel impossible.

But wait one moment—

Impossible until I suddenly remember:

I am alive,

I am alive,

I am alive,

And the recognition of the wondrousness of my life floods through me.

The life force that runs through my veins fills me with awe, and my totally unexpected story still amazes me.

Now, as I remember this, I know that I am likely to survive one more night.

As I snuggle deep into my bed under the soft down comforter, pondering this concept, my thoughts drift to a time when wondrousness consisted of losing myself under the gleaming stars in the night sky far from any city lights.

Fort Collins, Colorado, 1973

At first, everything seemed to flow so smoothly.

I had no idea that soon my world was going to fly apart and I would be ravaged by a rabid monster.

As a college freshman, my selection of Colorado State University in Fort Collins was solely based on the essential access I would have to the Rocky Mountains. In high school, I dreamed of escaping Texas. I felt like a wild ocelot dreaming of the day I could lose the bars of my cage and find my freedom. When I graduated from high school, my parents gave me the experience I had been craving: a thirty-five-day mountaineering expedition where I was trained in wilderness travel, including how to use an ice ax, pitons, crampons, and a climbing rope. This was essential knowledge I needed.

Arriving in Fort Collins, I couldn't wait to put on my heavy, clunky hiking boots, strap on my oversized olive green Kelty pack, and hitchhike as far as I could, catching a ride in the back of a pickup truck into the high country. I wasn't worried about hitchhiking or being alone in the wilderness; it was exactly the dream I'd played over and over while biding my time in San Antonio. All I had wanted was freedom—freedom from my parents, from the Texas heat and strip-mall landscape, and from the message the stunted trees and brown, sunburnt vegetation played over and over: It was 1973, and I was a prisoner in a land where I did not belong.

I was confident my real home was the wilderness. There had always been an aura of magic and promise about "going north." During high school, I devoured books about the ways of life, stories and beliefs of the ancient peoples, those indigenous tribes—the Hopi, the Navajo, the Cherokee, the Plains tribes, and so many others—who had rightly inhabited this land before they were so tragically and cruelly crushed. I valued the stories about how important it was for their young people to go on their vision quests, to get in touch with the roots of their existence, to see deeply into the meaning of their lives; these stories made so much sense to me, and inspired what I desired for myself. I knew with certainty this was essential for my life, too.

My first trip into the high country was exactly what I dreamed it would be: After my pickup truck ride, a retired couple drove me to a road head, and from there I was able to hike to a lake up near timberline. The rich texture of the dark green spruce trees, the silvery white bark of the aspen, the little chipmunks and marmots along the trail who chirped and whistled their greetings, and most of all, the infinite black night sky blazing with all the silver stars in heaven: this was precisely why I had come.

LATE SUNDAY, I SORROWFULLY MADE THE RETURN TRIP to my new home: a giant university and a women's dormitory called Parmalee Hall. I was in the cafeteria making a peanut butter sandwich, since I was too late for the regular dinner, when another resident approached me. She was about my height, which means she was short, and just like me, she wore her hair in a long braid down her back. We managed a nonchalant "hi," and I went back to focusing on my sandwich, but she had more to say.

"I saw you," she said, almost accusingly. "I saw you with your backpack. You were in the high country?"

"Yes," I said, hearing the excitement in my own voice. I had been up to Mummy Pass. It was fantastic. She responded, "I need you to teach me how to do this. I need to go there, too. That's why I'm here."

Again, I looked her over. I thought I was the only person in this big, impersonal university whose life depended on the wind-carved silence of the high country. Could it be she cared about this, too? After a few minutes of conversation, I realized I'd found a friend—my first and only friend there. Her name was Helen, and she had come from Ames, Iowa, for the same reason I had come from Texas: to get into the wilderness. And just like me, Helen was an art major. Together, we hatched a plan to go on the next trip into the wild together.

Before we could go into the wilderness, we needed to outfit her with all the necessary provisions: heavy leather boots, backpack, wool knickers—all just like my own— thick rag wool socks, a dark red wool ski sweater with the white shape of a deer leaping across her chest, a dark green Scottish wool tam-o'-shanter, and two metal canteens. We found most of these items at the Goodwill store, except for the boots and a lightweight down sleeping bag, which had to be purchased from the mountaineering shop. I showed her how to pack everything so it all fit neatly in her pack, except the sleeping bag, which had to be strapped to the pack's frame. We were ready, and when the weekend finally arrived, we were on our way out of town, hitchhiking down the road through Poudre Canyon.

That first trip was joyful. Two new friends, delighted with each other's company, thrilled to be surrounded by so much sheer beauty—we were hooked by this experience. We were in a state of perpetual awe. When it was time to head back to school, to Parmalee Hall, we were glum. This became our regular routine—packing up, donning our identical mountaineering "uniforms" and hitchhiking as far as we could possibly go on a Friday afternoon, imbibing the wildness, and then dolefully returning to the dorm at the end of the weekend. We purchased a small tent from the mountaineering store: a small, lightweight tent made just for backpacking.

Now we were prepared for anything!

Nearly.

EVERY THURSDAY AFTERNOON WE WOULD DUTIFULLY GO to art history class where images of famous paintings were projected vividly on the screen of the darkened auditorium-style classroom. It was a dreary autumn afternoon, and I was sitting in the back of the room, up high, in the otherwise empty back row. I didn't see Helen before class, so I was sitting by myself. The images of paintings by Spanish artist Francisco Goya were floating like colored birds, unmoored from any other living thing, in the vast darkness. I didn't recognize his paintings—The Black Paintings—but the violence, fear, and blood of the scenes permeated the room.

Then I heard it: a mumble, at first very faint, but growing louder. It was a voice, but I couldn't tell if it was male or female. I ignored it at first, but then I strained hard to understand the words it was repeating. Very faint at first, then growing louder, and suddenly I knew; it was intoning, "Bad, Bad, Bad!" I tried to disregard it, to focus harder on Goya's masterpieces, but this voice didn't care. And then I realized: this voice was issuing its judgment on my life. This voice spoke the truth. I wrapped my arms, hugging around myself, and waited for it to stop. Suddenly the lights came on, and I was back in the auditorium. The class was over now. The sounds of chairs and students' chatter replaced the intonations of the voice.

Still clutching myself, I rushed out the door.

I crossed the main plaza and struggled to get back to the dorm. The voices went with me. I saw another student, a girl, in a red sweater coming toward me, her blond ponytail bobbing up and down.

When she was closer, I looked at her face. To my horror, she didn't have a human face; instead, it was the face of a giant insect.

I rushed past her and finally arrived at my room. I went into the bathroom and looked at myself in the mirror.

Looking back was not my regular self; it was the countenance of an awful creature, with hot burning red eyes, black holes where the nose should have been, and where the mouth belonged, a dripping hole oozing red blood.

I knew at that moment, my life as I knew it was over.

I was now a beast.

THAT AUTUMN IN FORT COLLINS THE CRUEL VOICES I heard would not let me rest. It became apparent that only I heard them; no one else seemed to notice anything unusual. The voices taunted me, they condemned me, and there was no safe place I could hide. No place they couldn't find me. I tried to go to my classes, but it seemed impossible.

Helen knew something was happening to me, but I couldn't tell anyone—not even her. I wanted so badly to tell her what I was experiencing, but I knew it would scare her, and she wouldn't understand anyway.

No one would understand.

I was in this alone.

Just me and the cruel, inescapable voices.

The autumn progressed. The air suddenly became sharp and cold, and the sky filled with dense, navy blue clouds. The day had been so long; I felt exhausted from not being able to sleep and from having to be on guard constantly.

Then, just after daylight shifted into night, there was a miracle: tiny crystalline snowflakes began to fill the air—the first snow of the year.

I went out into the darkness and stood out underneath the streetlight, looking up.

The sky was filled with the most beautiful sight I'd ever seen—tiny swirling, dancing snowflakes. The voices condemned me, but the snow said, "*Aahhhhhhhhh…*"

I was utterly transfixed by the hypnotic scene. Here was relief. I could not move or stop my grateful gaze. I wanted to stay like this forever.

But then, some students came. They were gesturing at me; they were unhappy with me. I had neglected to wear my shoes or coat—such devices seemed irrelevant—and they seemed perplexed by it. They wanted me to go with them. I tried to point out to them how miraculous the snowflakes were—the beauty, the wonder.

"Look!—don't you see?!"

But, no, they didn't see it. They didn't understand. They were evidently upset with me, and I felt sorry I was bothering them. I didn't intend to make them unhappy. They emphatically insisted I go with them. I didn't want to, but I wanted to stop their unhappiness with me, so I finally gave in and went along with them. But to where? I didn't know or care.

I just wanted to be with the reassuring movement and soft feeling of the snow.

The student health center was a one-story, modern brick building. We went through the glass doors into the lobby with its orange plastic chairs and bright fluorescent lights. The students quickly left.

A woman, in white, escorted me to a small room with only a bed and a small table that had wheels. Her hair was piled on top of her head in a fantastic bun. How does she do that, I wondered.

It occurred to me she was possibly The Queen. What queen? I didn't know, but it seemed like a royal sign that her hair was up on top of her head. Just like a crown.

She gestured to me to remove my wet clothes, and when I didn't immediately respond, she roughly pulled them off me herself. She then wrapped a voluminous, pale green gown around me. I felt powerless to object.

This was such a strange place; why was I here?

Who was this queen person?

What was expected of me?

Another person in white appeared; in one hand she held a cup of water, and in the other, a tiny paper cup with two little pale-yellow pills.

"You must take these," she demanded. Her authority was inescapable.

I took the pills and swallowed them. They were bitter and stuck in my throat. But I did it. Then they motioned for me to get into the bed, so I did, and they pulled several thin blankets over me. Then they left the room, and it was just me, alone, with the voices shrilly laughing at me. I was so cold in those miserly thin blankets. I lay there, shaking and afraid, but then a profound sleepiness came over me; I could not resist it and fell into a deep, dreamless sleep.

———

I LOST TRACK OF TIME. OCCASIONALLY, ROYAL WOMEN in white would come into the room with more pills for me to take.

This was all there was: sleep, pills, sleep, pills, sleep, pills. I don't know how long this went on, but it seemed like days. Or years. It was timeless, and eventually I didn't care anymore. All I wanted was to sleep, to be left alone, and sleep, then sleep some more. The voices had stopped bothering me so much.

All I wanted was sleep.

———

SUDDENLY I WAS AWAKE. ONE OF THE ROYAL WOMEN IN white appeared.

"Lucky you, missy, now you get to see the psychiatrist." "The psychiatrist," she said, emphasizing this in a way that I knew it must be important. The way she said it made me feel a rush of dread. I had heard of psychiatrists before, but I knew nothing about what they did, except maybe they were some kind of doctor; a *shrink*, I thought they were called. I think maybe I saw one in a movie once—I couldn't remember. Was it like Sigmund Freud?

I was escorted down a long hall to the psychiatrist's office. I entered and heard the door squeak and then emphatically click behind me. It was a small office, filled up with a massive desk, tall shelves piled with books; and on the walls were myriad impressive framed diplomas and certificates.

And then, there he was.

The psychiatrist.

He motioned for me to sit.

And then I was able to get a full look at him. He was a big man, a little hunched over, and he looked ancient. His wild single tuft of hair was a yellowy-white. He had substantial bushy white eyebrows and, most remarkably, profuse untrimmed hair wiggled its way out his nose and ears. His eyes were watery blue and bloodshot. All I could do was stare at him and his prodigious nose hair.

We regarded each other, not speaking. Then he leaned toward me across his big desk and pointed his crooked old, decrepit, yellow finger at me. In a deep, accusatory voice, he intoned, "You have schizophrenia!!!"

I just sat there, stunned.

I had no idea what schizophrenia was, but I was sure that he had just given me a death sentence. It crossed my mind that anyone with that much nose hair couldn't possibly know what they were talking about.

But the power of his pronouncement was inescapable.

I was doomed.

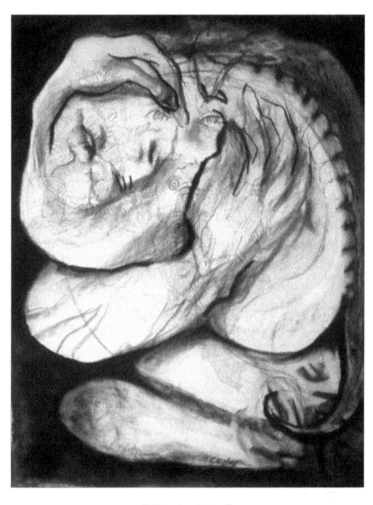

"Hugging Form"
Pen and ink on paper
30 x 40 in.

TWO

A forgotten language, spoken by the river,
spoken by the generations of river otters,
the drip, drip, drip, of the water in the dark
recesses of a cave—isn't this the song you were
singing to me—I heard it in my dreams
last night—were you there?

Portland, 2018

I'm never quite sure what to think about my life—so unpredictable—sometimes it's good, or even great, but then things crash down both inside and outside of me—and I'm desperately treading water in an endless turbulent ocean, trying not to drown.

It's Sunday morning in Portland, and I'm sitting on the edge of the sofa with Ananda in a rare sunny spot, reflecting on the week. The half-full cup of French roast sits forgotten.

On Thursday I met Maggie at the Vietnamese restaurant down the street from my office. Maggie is an unusual person I appreciate and admire. We're close friends, about the same age. She's a psychiatrist. She also has a background in literature, which means that she relates to things and ideas both as a scientist as well as a writer. She plays a unique role in my life. She is the person who has agreed to be my representative on my advance directive. This means that if I were to botch a suicide attempt and was left brain-dead, Maggie would be the one with the legal authority to tell them to pull the plug. It's a dark thought. I know this seems grim, but these are the things one thinks about when one is living on the very jagged edge of the world. She and I have discussed this in detail, and I know she is willing to carry out my wishes.

This is an enormous thing to be willing to do. I don't take it lightly, and I know that Maggie doesn't either. I can be completely honest with her.

She makes it clear she wants me to stay alive.

Let there be no mistake about it.

And I don't want to let her down.

Over sautéed spicy vegetables she asks me if I plan to get another dog after Ananda, my Lhasa apso, is gone. Maggie always surrounds herself with people, horses, and dogs, and I know she believes in having a newer, younger dog so that when the older one dies, she isn't left bereft; there is still a dog there to be a comfort. So, she asks me the sixty-four-million-dollar question: Will I get another dog? No, I reply. After mother goes and Ananda goes, I won't have anything holding me on the planet.

I know this isn't what she wants to hear, but I'm trying to be honest, both to her and myself. And yet, we both know I have a strong life force—this is unquestionable.

Ananda is probably close to sixteen years old—I don't know her exact age, but I got her from the animal shelter about twelve years ago. Lhasa apsos are descended from the Himalayan wolf, but she is small and looks nothing like a wolf. She had been found tied to a tree, wearing a pink coat that read "Princess." Someone had tied her up and left her there. They didn't go back.

I suspect someone loved her but for some unhappy reason could not keep her. They tied her to the tree, so she wouldn't run out into the traffic. They were hoping someone would find her and take her home and love her. I wish I could tell them what a happy life she has now. I love her so much. Maggie loves Ananda, too, and Ananda loves Maggie. When I was in the psych hospital, Maggie kept her, and she slept on Maggie's bed with Maggie's three other dogs and one husband. It must have been very cozy.

I dread the day when I have to say goodbye to Ananda.

Sometimes I reach down to the foot of my bed in the middle of the night, to feel her soft fur and let her know I love her. It is impossible to imagine living without her. She is officially my service dog, and she goes with me everywhere, including to the office every weekday.

I realize most dogs usually don't live much longer than fourteen or fifteen years. My former dear old Tibetan terrier, Iris, lived to be just over fifteen years old. She was well-loved. The last few years of her life, I had birthday parties for her, and everyone who loved her came to celebrate her life. The house overflowed with lots of adoring people, and I would fill all the rooms and even the porch with purple irises; they were everywhere.

Lately, I've been thinking I need to start having birthday parties for Ananda. In April, a month from now, it will be the anniversary of her coming to live with me, of us being together, faithful and true. I must plan a party. I will have the party to honor the day we found each other. There are so many people who love her. I will send out invitations with her picture, or maybe an oil crayon drawing. We will have a bursting full house, everyone celebrating her remarkable life.

I say to Maggie that when Ananda is gone, won't it be natural for me to follow her, to wherever that may be? My brother and father both died at an age not much older than I am now.

As I say this to Maggie, I watch her expression. She is careful not to judge me or push back too hard. I know in the back of her mind she is thinking about what it would be like for her if I decide to die by my own hand, sooner rather than later. What will her role be? What will be her responsibilities in knitting up the details I leave behind?

She and I both understand this, and neither of us wants it.

Maggie shares how she has a friend in the Netherlands who is also a psychiatrist and who is a proponent of euthanasia for some mental health conditions, such as depression and bipolar disorder. This psychiatrist-friend asked Maggie if there had ever been patients whom she had not been able to help. Maggie answered honestly: yes. Then, said the Dutch psychiatrist, wouldn't it be better to be able to offer them relief from their suffering? Maggie said she wasn't sure, and I can tell this thought is problematic to ponder. Maggie is willing to ask herself this hard question, even when she doesn't seem to have a ready answer.

When lunch is over, on our way out of the restaurant we stop at the counter and get peppermints because our meal has been full of garlic. We give each other a long hug before going back to our respective offices. I am an anomaly in Maggie's life, and she is also an anomaly in mine. But we are important to each other.

Later I get a message from her telling me that I am "a treasure." And I treasure her. Our lives are so different, yet here we are, two women whose paths touch and affect each other. To each other we are essential.

And just knowing her and having her for a friend makes it somehow easier to stay on the planet.

Colorado, 1974-1975

I was being torn into jagged fragments, even though I tried to proceed with my life.

My freshman year in college was marked by fervent backpacking trips into the wilderness punctuated by stolid overnight stays at the student health center. They would give me the little pale-yellow pills that made me so sleepy, and I would sleep for a few days in a darkened room. And somehow in the middle of this pattern, I would go to my classes. I dropped most of them except drawing and art history.

Even my drawing class was challenging. The instructor filled the floor in the center of the classroom with a pile of various cold, unfeeling objects: shiny metal car fenders, variously colored glass bottles, different shapes and sizes of cardboard boxes, including an empty box of oatmeal, an alarm clock, unidentifiable machine parts, a basketball, eye-glasses. These objects had no meaning for me; they lacked any relationship to nature. No plants, nothing growing, no stones, no animals, no nests of animals, no antlers, no feathers, no leaves, no stumps, no seeds, no sign of any living thing. There was nothing in the center of the classroom to which I could relate. Instead, the artificial, lifeless objects symbolized the synthetic, impoverished, sharp-edged reality that I was fighting against. The assignment was to draw the lifeless, meaningless forms. This was supposed to be a class about making art, but it seemed like just another expression of my alienation from everything in the dispiriting university environment.

I sat on the floor of the classroom and drew my memories and impressions from the previous weekend's snowshoeing trip, oblivious to the instructor's unsympathetic collection of objects in front of me. The instructor would occasionally stand behind me, his arms crossed, and silently observe my blatant noncompliance. He didn't say anything or acknowledge I wasn't doing the assignment. A small but appreciated grace. I was engrossed in my rebellious drawings, grateful to be left alone.

IN MY FREQUENT TRIPS TO THE STUDENT HEALTH CENTER, I got to know Sam, the woman who sat at the reception desk. She was young, with long dark hair and a warm expression. She always smiled and acted like she was genuinely glad to see me.

She invited me to visit her goat farm, just outside town. It became one of the few places I felt safe. I would ride my red, rusty bicycle out from the city to her place, and soon I knew all the goats' names. Her favorite goat was Emily. Sam put a big rubber nozzle on a Coke bottle filled with milk, then I would offer it to the hungry little kid goats, whose little tails would wag at fifty-thousand miles per minute as they gulped it down. They would jump on top of one another vying for a drink. As I watched them, I saw how they were filled with life and gusto. I wondered where their enthusiasm for life came from. Was their behavior joy, or was it desperation? I realized it was a joyous dance of life.

Sometimes I would visit the goat farm even when Sam wasn't there. We had an agreement that I could go up into the loft of the barn if I needed to be in a place that felt safe. Sitting on the fragrant straw, up high, I watched the particles of dust playing through the slanted yellow shafts of sunlight. Down below the loft were the chickens, whose cozy murmurs and occasional squawks were soothing and hypnotic.

Here I felt safe.

I clung to every little sunlit detail.

There was one other place where I could go and feel safe: The "Goose Refuge." Bobby, the older brother of a friend from high school, lived in a little shack on a wild piece of land just outside town. Bobby was studying to get his doctorate in some obscure subject that I knew nothing about. All I knew was that he would happily make me a cup of peppermint tea with honey if I showed up when he was there, and if he wasn't there, I was welcome to let myself in and make the cup of tea myself. His door was never locked. Not too far from the shack was the goose pond.

The pond wasn't too big—just a body of water surrounded by wild fields of high, pale golden grass, scrub vegetation, and occasional clusters of dark trees that had lost their leaves. Sometimes there was a dusting of snow and a thin layer of ice on the pond where the water was shallow. There was a scant path that led to a place on the bank of the pond where a small wooden raft was moored. The raft was only about six or seven feet square. There was a long stout pole that was always within reach.

I would gently step onto the raft, with my backpack and with my sleeping bag, and as the night drew near, I would unroll my sleeping bag and, if it wasn't too cold, lie on top of it as the currents carried us randomly across the surface of the pond. If it was really cold, I would crawl in and burrow inside it.

Sometimes I would observe a muskrat swimming smoothly along, but I was mostly alone. When dark night was drawing near, the wild geese would start to come, to roost along the banks for the night. They would squawk loudly as they settled down, more than a hundred of them. The twilight would grow dimmer, and night would turn the sky from a pale lavender to an ever-deeper shade of purple. I would lie on top of my sleeping bag until it got too cold, and then I would crawl inside. All night I would float randomly across the surface of the pond. It would be quiet, and then something unseen would alert the geese and they would suddenly raise their voices, squawking in a chorus, until they eventually settled back down into silence. Just the lapping of the water on the raft, and on the banks of the pond. I would look up at the stars, vast and silent, and even though the cruel voices in my head would often intrude, I was able to find some semblance of peace. When early morning was close, a grey mist formed across the surface of the pond. Then, as if it had been choreographed, all at once, in total unison, the geese would suddenly begin flapping their great wings, and honking, and all together, would rise up into the air and take to flight. There was the sound of their honking voices mixed with the sound of their wings thrashing against the air. It was thundering loud, and I witnessed it with total reverence. And then at once they would regally fly away, not to return again until dusk.

Eventually I would use the pole to guide the raft back to the bank, pack up my sleeping bag, hop on my bicycle and pedal back to the university. I was always grateful for this experience, and even though the voices didn't totally leave me alone, their grip was loosened.

BUT I WASN'T REALLY SAFE.

I wish the reality and safe feeling of life in the hay loft and the goose refuge was all that I would remember from that year.

I had no idea what would happen next.

IT WAS AFTER THE SPRING SEMESTER THAT I FOUND myself back in San Antonio. I had not succeeded in my year at the university in Fort Collins. I had to realize my year of trips into the mountains with my backpack was not the answer I had hoped it would be. The goose refuge and Sam's goat farm did not save me. I couldn't totally understand what happened.

The voices and the dark side of my world grew even more immense. It was obvious to my parents and to everyone who knew me that I was in deep trouble. My parents turned to a local psychiatrist for advice. He was adamant in his pronouncement: I must be hospitalized right away in a psychiatric hospital. And according to him, the best place in Texas for this to happen was the hospital in Galveston.

In less than a week, I found myself admitted to this huge hospital: an imposing modern building where the lobby was decorated with glass and gleaming chrome. The walls were painted a shiny, lacquered black. I immediately observed the irony of painting the walls black in a hospital where people were trying to heal from depression and hopelessness.

The one good thing was I was free to come and go. At least at first. On my second day there, I left the hospital and walked directly to the nearby convenience store. I purchased a six pack of lukewarm Miller High Life beer. I wasn't much of a drinker, but I hoped that by drinking this six pack I might feel better. I proceeded to sit down at a nearby bus stop and drink three of the cans. On the third can I was feeling terrible, but dizzy-good at the same time. My psychic pain was like a noose—but a little looser around my neck.

I choked down one more can, then staggered back to the psychiatric inpatient unit.

Immediately, when the nurses saw me, they sprang into action, gathered my inebriated self up, and sent me in a windowless white van to the "closed unit."

Even in my drunken state, I immediately realized that I was now in a place where I wouldn't be able to leave: the doors slammed shut behind me, and many badges and keys had to be produced in order to go in or out of them.

Although the first hospital had been gleaming new chrome and modern design, this hospital was an ancient, craggy, tan brick building that looked like a fortress about to collapse on itself.

And the name:

It was called Graves.

Honestly.

So, help me, God.

Here I was.

Locked up in Graves.

Soon, it didn't really matter. The voices started howling at me. All I could do was lie in my bed in my little dingy room and hold tight to the pillow, as if it were a life raft in a fierce storm. The nurses injected me with their medicine, but the voices didn't care. I could only hold on for my life, and there were no guarantees that I would make it through.

The war that was being waged inside my head was terrifying. I didn't know where I was, and I didn't care. I lay curled up in my bed and was not aware of time passing or anything else. It was a moment-to-moment question of whether I would be able to survive.

At one point I realized that sitting in a chair next to my bed was a person in a white jacket: one of the doctors. She silently regarded me with both fear and clinical curiosity. It didn't make any difference to me she was there. My war continued.

Eventually I uncurled myself just enough so I could look at her. To my horror, over her head, the air was filling up with gigantic, black flying spiders, each bigger than my hand. They were quickly filling the room, all the way up to the ceiling. More and more of them, and soon they were spinning everyplace; the air was thick with them.

Why doesn't she do anything about this?! Doesn't she see what's happening?! Can't she do something to make them go away?!

A nurse gave me another injection.

The horrible scene gave way to unconsciousness.

AFTER A FEW DAYS OF SLEEPING ON AND OFF, SOMETHING new happened. It was very early in the morning, still dark. An orderly smelling of cigarettes showed up beside my bed with a wheelchair. Once I got in it, he pushed me down a hall to the elevator. Even in my altered state, I knew this was an elevator like one from out of an old movie. It had bars across the door that had to be opened like an accordion.

We got on, and with the elevator moaning and vibrating, we went down, down, down. To the basement.

Down to the bowels of Graves.

I was told to sit on a long, shiny blue leatherette couch. White stuffing, like wayward sheep, protruded from one of the blue leatherette arms. The floor was a peeling, washed-out green linoleum. I observed it with detachment. It seemed to be consistent with the general air of dissolution that was everywhere at Graves.

I SAT THERE AS I HAD BEEN TOLD TO DO AND STARTED to wake up more. Next to me, sitting just as quietly, were two other patients. We didn't say a word or even acknowledge one another.

I grew more and more concerned about what was going to happen. I observed the male orderly appear in the door and motion to them, one by one. Without a word, they would stand up and follow him to another room.

After a while I was sitting there by myself. No one told me what this was about, and my tense questioning grew. After a long wait, the orderly appeared and motioned for me to follow him. I stood up slowly, adjusting to being on my feet. I followed him to a large, bright room furnished with gurneys and imposing, strange grey metal box-like machines.

I was led to a gurney next to one of the big square machines. It had gauges, buttons, dials, and lots of wires and cables. There were several nurses and a doctor standing there. They wordlessly motioned for me to get aboard the gurney.

I started to feel strong foreboding and dread to see

what was going to happen next. I lay there passively as I was strapped down. One strap around each of my ankles, one around my lower legs, then my thighs, across my chest, each arm, until they got to my head. The doctor wordlessly reached over and firmly took my lower jaw in his surprisingly soft hands.

"Open!" he sternly commanded.

I opened my mouth, and he quickly stuck in a big, dry, unfamiliar angular object; I felt like I was going to gag, and I tried to scream NO!

But then nothing.

Absolutely nothing.

⸺◦⸺

THE NEXT THING I KNEW, I WAS LYING ON A GURNEY IN a different room. At first, I just lay there, barely awake, but gradually I awakened more and turned my head so I could see where I was. There was a line of gurneys, just like mine; some were empty, but some had patients in them—I figured they must be sleeping or dead because no one moved.

I knew I should just stay put and wait to see what would happen next. I felt strangely like my body wasn't really there. I tested one foot, and then the other, and found they both were still attached and were able to move. Next my hands, they could move too. I was faintly relieved. Things seemed hazy.

After an endless span of time, an orderly came and told me to get up and follow him. I slowly, unsteadily climbed down off the gurney. He led me into yet another room with a long, wooden table. Patients were quietly sitting in plastic chairs in front of the table, and there were big bowls of anemic scrambled eggs and grey, oily grits. Mechanically, the patients were spooning the cold eggs and grits into their mouths. I sat on the end and followed the others.

Cold scrambled eggs. Cold mealy grits.

We ate, in silence.

Finally, I was taken back to my room in a wheelchair. I went to sleep and slept for the rest of the day.

Early the next morning, in the dark, the cigarette-smelling orderly appeared again at my bedside. The wheelchair, the creaky elevator, the blue leatherette couch, the strapping down of my arms and legs—everything was the same as the day before.

When the doctor told me to open my mouth, I tried to scream NO, but as I opened my mouth, in went the terrible, hulking object.

Then darkness.

JUST AS THE DAY BEFORE, I AWOKE, GROGGY, IN THE other room. I tested my feet and hands, to see if they could move, and eventually was led into the room with the silent row of patients, mechanically eating the cold scrambled eggs.

Finally, back to my room, escaping to the darkness of sleep.

Day after day, this same eerie scene was repeated. This routine became my life. Every day was the same. Over and over. A young medical student named Terry, who sometimes visited me, and always wore a bow tie with his white doctor's coat, told me it was electric shock treatment. I did not really understand or care. It was so predictable.

Every day. Down to the bowels of Graves. Struggle. Darkness. Nothing mattered.

ONE STRANGE THING, THOUGH: EVERY EVENING, BEFORE they brought the nightly medications, they brought me a letter in a pale blue envelope. I would shakily open it, and it always said sentences that made no sense, then it was signed, "Love, Helen."

Helen? Who was this? I didn't have a clue. I would put the letter carefully back into the light blue envelope and then put it along with the other identical light blue envelopes on the windowsill. All from someone named Helen, but I didn't know a Helen; who was she? Like everything else, it made no sense.

Nothing made sense anymore. Somehow my memories of my time in Colorado had simply disappeared. I was a person without a history.

The voices in my head grew quiet. Actually, I didn't really have many thoughts at all. There was nothing expected of me except the repetition of passively going in the wheelchair early every morning and then the rest of the day blurred into nothingness.

One morning when the orderly with the wheelchair appeared, he told me that I was not going to the bowels of Graves for the usual electric shock treatment. He said I was going to be taken to a different part of the hospital for a different kind of shock.

He pushed me in the wheelchair to a waiting white van. I was loaded in, and it took me to a modern building nearby. I was taken into an unfamiliar room where there was just one bed. A nurse put an IV into my arm. I didn't know what would happen next. A doctor appeared.

"Just relax," he commanded in a tone that was very unrelaxing.

I lay there; there was nothing else for me to do.

And then nothing.

Everything went dark.

When I awoke I felt groggy and dazed. I couldn't understand what had happened. The nurse appeared and handed me a tall glass of orange juice to drink. She commanded me to drink it. I tentatively took a sip. It was unexpectedly sweet—sickeningly so—this glass of orange juice had at least half a cup of sugar added to it. I hesitated, not wanting it, but the nurse sternly instructed me to drink it up. She stood there watching me like a hawk as I choked it down and did not leave until I'd finished the last drop.

Then I was taken in the wheelchair back to the van, then back to the locked ward of Graves. Later that day, Terry the medical student visited me. I struggled to interact with him.

I asked him what had happened to me, and he said that it was a different kind of shock treatment called "insulin coma treatment." He said the reason I had to drink the sweetened orange juice was to help bring me back from the coma. He emphasized the word *coma*. It filled me with fear, but then I decided that it was better to get this insulin coma shock treatment than the electroshock because it was in a newer place, much more pleasant than the bowels of Graves.

After that first morning, each morning alternated between the electroshock at Graves and the trip in the van to the modern place for insulin coma shock.

The balding middle-aged psychiatrist was mostly absent during my time in the hospital, but one day he appeared and asked me a strange question, He asked, "Do you see me as an authority figure?"

I pondered it for a minute, then replied, "Can you fly?"

He looked truly puzzled and said, "No."

"Then I guess you're not an authority figure," I answered.

One afternoon, after weeks of the intensive treatments, the same psychiatrist, who was certainly no authority figure, appeared and happily announced to me that I had made progress.

Progress?

What progress?

I could hardly say my name.

My mind was like it had been wiped away and only my body remained as an inert shell.

There wasn't much left of me.

My parents came to take me home to San Antonio. It had been six months since I was free. As we drove through the countryside, I greedily took in the miraculous sights of cows, cars, cactuses, billboards, and buildings. My senses began to reopen. I rolled down the window of the car and felt the wind on my face. The fragrance of the fields, of living beings awakened me.

It was beautiful, although I felt shame and failure to be returning to San Antonio.

When we arrived home, I rushed upstairs to the bedroom that I had known since high school. I opened the door and was struck by the brilliance of the bright sunflower yellow painted walls and matching yellow shag carpet. I had the thought that Vincent Van Gogh would approve of these walls. Vincent Van Gogh would have known how I felt. He would have been my comrade, my brother.

But now, was there any possibility of hope? Did I dare?

"Pain Cry"
Pen and ink on paper
18 x 24 in.

THREE

Her breath curled through the air making circles
around her head, like an acanthus garland,
so hard won, yet so easy, and when they spoke
to her, softly asking the directions to her hiding
place, she pulled back in the dense dark shell
which, like the body of a turtle, engulfed her
white body—oh who are you anyway,
they called out in exasperation, but the circle
around her head rolled heavily down over
her eyes, and then I realized she was gone.

Portland, 2018

Sometimes it seems like I can try and get by, but other times, things swell up into impossibility.

Tonight, here in Portland, I went to yoga class. Ananda was with me, wearing her purple vest that says, "Service Dog," tethered by her leash to a metal folding chair next to my mat. I was doing the posture affectionately called "Downward Facing Dog" on my hands and feet with my rump up in the air and my face looking down at the floor when I spied the tiniest dark ant twaddling in zigzags across the cork floor. I became frantic as I tried to catch it and save it from getting stepped on, a certain death. But as soon as

I had found a piece of paper, so I could safely scoop it up, the little thing was gone.

I did not succeèd in saving it.

There was a woman in the corner of the room struggling to get into the awkward poses; her frustration and unhappiness was obvious. After a while she gave up and quickly put her things away, and then walked out the door. I jumped up and hurried out to find her, hoping that I might save her from feeling bad by commending her for her efforts and encouraging her with my own story of how hard it used to be, but then how it got better.

She was already gone.

I did not succeed in saving her.

Finally, as I was twisted into a convoluted pose, I asked myself why I feel such a strong need to save all these beings tonight. It occurred to me that I am really the one who needs saving.

I have been obsessing about death a lot lately—about Ananda's eventual death, about my mother's eventual death, and about how, when they are gone, I will be free to end my own life. I need saving from myself and the doom of my own mind…to save myself from myself somehow.

On the way home from class, I stopped by the variety store and bought a bird feeder and a bag of thistle seed, so I could save the hungry little birds. Then I realized I had not had dinner myself, so here was yet one more example of me trying to save the beings of the world while being so out of touch with my own need.

On the way out of the store I saw a cluster of Girl Scouts by the door selling their cookies to shoppers going in and out. I did not want any cookies, but as I drove away, I fantasized about going back, buying a box and then giving it back to them with the instruction that they were to give it as a gift to the saddest looking person they could find.

So now it is nearly time to go to bed.

I have not saved a single being today.

I remember that as a little girl my hero was Mighty Mouse because he saved everyone, even though he was only a very small mouse. I thought if I could just be like him then I might be able to save everyone from the sadness and unhappiness that surrounds us. He was very small, but he could do anything that needed to be done. Mighty Mouse could fly, he was immensely strong, and he cared about all the people in distress. I loved him fiercely for it.

Now I have taken my nightly medication and four melatonin tablets. I have donned my soft blue nightgown with hopes that somehow, I will be relieved of these thoughts by the deep release of sleep.

Maybe Mighty Mouse will visit me in my dreams. Maybe tonight he will be the one who saves me.

Maybe.

San Antonio, Texas, 1976-1978

I was like a swimmer who had been sucked out into the deep ocean and was trying to stay afloat even though the cold waters dragged me down and filled my lungs with lead.

I was back in San Antonio and enrolled at the Trinity University. Every day I would drive the old green Volkswagen to the university parking lot and struggle to walk across campus to my classes. The schizophrenia medication I took every morning and night made it very hard to walk like a regular person. I was a zombie, an automaton. My arms and legs felt frozen. They didn't want to cooperate with me. I didn't want to stand out from everyone else, so I battled to swing my arms back and forth like a normal person walking. Left arm forward, then back, right arm forward, then back, over and over, move one foot, then the other, I awkwardly stumbled along. When I was in the hospital, I had learned that walking this way, because of the medication side effects, was called "the Thorazine Shuffle." I really didn't want this to be me, so I tried really hard to walk like everyone else. It wasn't easy.

In my Spanish class we had an exam. The handsome young professor placed the blank test face down on my desk. I picked it up and looked at it. The words swam on the page, grey and fuzzy. I couldn't read any of the words—my eyes didn't work right. I had never had this problem before. My eyesight had always been very clear. I sat there panicked. The schizophrenia medication had made my vision all blurry, and I couldn't see well enough to read. What could I do? I couldn't read it at all. I was stuck. Trapped.

Finally, I got up and walked to the front of the class, where the professor was sitting, and placed my blank test on the desk in front of him. He looked up at me questioningly. I said nothing but walked out the door. I felt defeated and any hope I might have had simply disappeared into the murky air.

So, this was how I proceeded through school: the medication would have severe side effects that made it impossible to do the things I, as a student, had to do. I became deeply frustrated and discouraged, so I would stop taking the medication. When I stopped taking it, my vision would clear up, my hands would stop shaking, and I would be able to see and walk like a regular person, but the volume of my internal voices would grow so loud I couldn't focus on anything but them. When the voices took control of my mind, I would be sent to the county psychiatric hospital, where they would force me to go back on the medication. I tried to refuse, but it was no use; they insisted I take it. If I refused, they held me down on the bed and gave me an injection in my butt. After all, they had the power and authority; I was just a patient. It was made very clear to me that patients had no say in what happened to them. The doctors and nurses had all the power. I was a voiceless captive.

The pattern of going off and on medication and in and out of the hospital became the rhythm of how I went through school. This sad pattern left me deeply unhappy. I started to think about ending my life. There was just so much unhappiness, and less and less did it seem worth it. I struggled to attend my classes. I switched my major from art to psychology so I could try to understand what was happening to my brain. My will to live started to ebb away.

I asked a young professor if I could do an independent study in suicidology: the technical term for the study of suicide. When he agreed, I started reading every possible book and medical journal on suicide. I was actually getting college credit for obsessing about killing myself.

The irony of this was hard to reconcile.

I was unhappy living at home with my parents. It was just another way in which my being a failure was obvious. I wasn't a child—why should I have to live with my parents and conform to their narrow and objectionable expectations? After many discussions, I convinced them to let me move out from home to the dormitory. In order to do so, I had to officially meet with the dean of students. Apparently, she controlled everything about who lived in the dorms and various rooms on campus. I would have to go along with this procedure of her interviewing me if I were to be allowed to live in one of the dorms. It was a compromise to follow this procedure, but I would do it even though I felt like rebelling.

I had never talked with or even met a dean before, and I was apprehensive as I approached the Dean's Office. I sat in the waiting room until a woman came out and introduced herself as Peg, the dean. I looked up at her and was surprised to see she was young and pretty. I had expected an old, gray, intimidating person. Peg wasn't like that at all.

I followed her to her office, trying to absorb the strange and unexpected experience.

In her office there were little candles flickering every-where, and a Hindu OM sign was hanging across the window.

I surely didn't predict this!

We started to talk, and she asked me why I wanted to move into the dorm. I felt surprisingly at ease talking with her—she seemed kind and genuinely interested in my answers. I told her what it was like for me to take medications that made it nearly impossible to do my studies. I told her about the trips to the hospital and how much of a struggle it was to be at school. She gently asked more questions, and I started to feel like I was talking to a real human being who could understand what I was dealing with. At the end of an hour and a half, I was so surprised to feel like I had made a new friend. She told me about the dorm room she was going to assign me, and she gave me a shiny new brass key. I left her office feeling hopeful and upbeat.

I went straight to the dorm and used my new key to let myself into my new home. The first thing I noticed was the room was painted a blaring shade of pink that looked like the medicine one takes for an upset stomach. But I was happy to have a new place other than my parents' house to call home. Later I met my new roommate, Carla from Nebraska. She was friendly and didn't ask many questions. I decided it was going to work out.

The next week, I started to get into a bad state. I had stopped taking my medications because of how hard they were making it for me to function as a student. The voices started growing louder and louder. I lay in my bed, in the pink dorm room, with the voices screaming at me, obscuring everything else. I no longer knew where I was, or anything else, except that the voices were trying to tear me apart. This battle went on and on. Then I vaguely became aware of the presence of another being—a human being—sitting next to me. At first, I didn't recognize her, but it was Peg, the dean. But now she seemed different somehow. I had a new sense of being safe with her being there right next to me. A realization occurred to me that she and I had known each other for many lifetimes before this. Slowly, the voices started to lose their hold on me. I opened my eyes and saw her face. I recognized her, but her name was no longer Peg: her new name, from the dark world I had just been in, was "Setanva." This name meant that she was a protector from another space and time. She reached over and took my hand.

I tentatively said her new name, *Setanva*, to her, and she calmly nodded her head in affirmation.

I now had a new ally named Setanva.

With Setanva's help I managed to make it through school. Whenever I got in trouble, whether with an unsympathetic professor or with more voices, she seemed to be able to save me. Somehow, with her help, I made it through one semester after another.

And then it was finally time to graduate—a truly a profound surprise. It was kind of like witnessing a stunning, unexplained lunar object that had fallen unexpected out of the sky.

It was the night of the commencement. I had on my cap and gown. When my name was called, I awkwardly walked across the stage and received my diploma. It felt like I was a sea creature that had walked out of the ocean onto the strange land for the first time. I knew I had just squeaked by, but it was a miracle nonetheless. After the ceremony when all the new graduates shifted our tassels to the other side of our mortarboards, I walked out of the auditorium, into the darkness. Waiting there at the curb, in the dark, was my father. He had come all the way from Shreveport, Louisiana, to see his daughter graduate. I had not seen him in years, and I was immediately struck by how small he was. Instead of a suit and tie, he was wearing a tan windbreaker.

"Pop! You came!" I cried. We hugged for a long time, and he congratulated me. He said he was proud of me. I was stunned. These priceless words meant everything—I had actually made my father proud. The struggle had all been worth it.

Plainfield, Vermont, 1978

I tried to hold on to some semblance of hope and encouragement, but the monsters within my mind would only make a mockery of my efforts.

I arrived in Plainfield, Vermont, to attend graduate school at Goddard College. I wanted to become an art therapist. I thought it would be the perfect thing for me to do since it combined psychology with art.

Arriving a few days before school started, I hitchhiked with my backpack over to New Hampshire to explore the White Mountains. The world seemed optimistic as I embarked on this new endeavor. I looked around me at the infinite shades of green in the landscape and my heart was light. Thank goodness I was not in Texas. The many varieties of green foliage suited me, and I knew I was in the right place.

A beat-up sedan stopped to give me a ride right away. It was a youngish man with a Yankees baseball hat and an orangey-red unshaven face. We drove into the steep mountains of New Hampshire, to a dramatically verti-cal passage called Crawford Notch, and into the heart of a ferocious thunderstorm. The rain grew heavier and heavier. The windshield wipers were having trouble keep-ing up with the pounding volumes of water assaulting us. The sounds of thunder crescendoed and bounced off the mountains that surrounded us. The downpour intensified even more, and the driver finally had to pull off to the side of the road, as it was no longer possible to see through the windshield.

We sat there, watching and listening to the fierce storm.

"I could give you some real excitement," the driver said. "I need some pussy real bad."

I sat there, unmoving. I thought I heard what he said, and I thought I knew what he meant.

Here was this vast storm going on, and here I was in the middle of the White Mountains. With this awful psy-chopath.

Oh shit.

I would either get out of the car right then, or—

Or what?

I turned and glared at him as sturdy and tough as I knew how.

"Listen, buddy, you're going to drive me to the next town. And that's all. Get it?"

He looked angry, but finally nodded in agreement, and his hands stayed on the wheel.

We sat for a little while in strained silence and finally the rain slacked off.

When it was clear enough to drive, he started the car back up and without a word we made it to the next town. He stopped at the first red light. I jumped out of the car and slammed the door behind me.

I didn't look back.

I went into a café to get some turkey sandwiches to take on my backpacking trip. The women behind the counter wanted to know why I needed five turkey sandwiches. I told them about the adventure upon which I had embarked. A waitress said, "Aren't you afraid of bears?"

"No! But I'm afraid of people!"

A WEEK LATER I WAS AT GODDARD COLLEGE AND CLASSES were about to start. Gladys, the director of the master's program, was a painter as well as an art therapist. She had an ageless, mischievous countenance and red hair. I liked her. She didn't seem like the dictator type.

Half the classes would be lecture and half would be experiential: making art. In the first class, after the orientation duties, we learned to do what were called "free drawings." I took big pieces of paper and colored oil pastels in many brilliant colors. The idea was to draw without thinking about it. Just let the hand go wherever it wanted, without any plan or thoughts.

No judgments, no preferences. The rational mind was irrelevant. My subconscious took the lead.

I didn't think at all about what I was going to draw; I concentrated on the emotional feelings in my core. My inner energy, with its wisdom and passion, surged forth.

I let my hand go where it wanted to go on the paper.

My energy expanded. I loosened up and started to draw faster and faster.

Lines and swirls of color, images, jagged, sharp.

The paper occasionally ripped from the force of my marks.

As I finished one drawing, it would fall out of the way onto the floor, and I would immediately start another, and then another.

Lots of black, red, yellow, a jab of blue.

Sometimes there were recognizable shapes: a tree, a panther, lightning strikes.

Sometimes it was just patterns of energy—energy coming off the sun, shooting through the universe.

I could do this forever. This was much more important than everything else.

We were told to take sketchbooks back to the dorm and draw regularly.

This way of drawing had opened something up inside me, inside my mind, inside my deepest psyche.

My subconscious was gaping open, and its contents were now pouring out.

I WENT TO THE COLLEGE HEALTH CENTER AND TOLD them that I might need to get some medication for my mental health condition. I was not very enthusiastic or convincing. They did not seem to think I had a problem either; they thought maybe I was malingering, just pretending I had an ailment so I could get drugs. Eventually, they grudgingly gave me some Thorazine, which was very familiar to me by then. I didn't really want it; it just seemed like the proper thing to do.

The voices were bothering me big time.
High-pitched wailing.
You should kill yourself!
I left the dorm.
Walked past the classrooms to the trail into the dense forest.
Off the trail.
Up into the woods.

I was running now.
Trying to get away.
Away from the noise.
Branches of trees scraped my face and body.
I kept going.
The forest was thick, and I slowed down.
I was very alone.
The voices started to let up.
I came to a little clearing where there was a circle of young pine trees.
Pine needles covered the ground.
Since I had been awake for many hours, I lay down on the forest floor and curled up into a ball.
My long hair was loose and fell around me onto the ground.
I was aware of lying there for a long, long time.

I might have slept; I didn't know. There was no sense of time passing. I was simply there with the young trees and an occasional squirrel.

The voices had become quiet.

I finally sat up and tried to compose myself.

I tried to smooth my hair; it was all in disarray.

I touched it, and in the long strands my hands felt strange, little foreign objects that were cold, moist and sticky.

Squishy.

In my hair!

I didn't want to touch them. They felt awful.

But I did it. I had to do it.

Carefully.

One, by one. My hair was full of these strange things!

I jumped to my feet and started to run in panic—I had to get away from them!

But when I ran, of course, my hair went with me, on my head. It was impossible to get away from my hair.

I realized this pretty quickly.

I stopped.

Somehow, I connected with reality.

With a jolt of shock, I realized these things in my hair were little slugs.

In reality, my hair was full of these soft, little, grey slugs.

These innocent little animals had come up from the forest floor.

Now they were burrowed all throughout my hair. Probably to them my hair seemed like a good place for baby slugs to spend the afternoon.

I could not run away from them.

I would have to be calm.

I would have to pick them out. It was a matter of fact.

So, I picked them out.

No voices then.
    Just slugs.
    It took forever to get them all out. One by one.
    Slug therapy.
    Not recommended, but it works.

I was at the lecture on psychopharmacology given to my class by a psychiatrist. He was talking about all the drugs used to treat the various mental illnesses. Nobody in my program knew that I had been diagnosed with schizophrenia, except Gladys, the director. The doctor told the class what the maximum dose of Thorazine is for someone who is hospitalized. I was sitting there in the class, on a dose higher than the maximum dose he had just told us.
    I wanted to raise my hand and say:
    Correction, Doctor!
    Correction!
    But I was quiet.
    It did give me pause.

Another class, and we were looking at artwork done by mentally ill patients, trying to determine their diagnosis just by looking at their drawings. I was unusually good at this. I could make the correct diagnosis, and somehow, I even could tell the age, gender, and other things about the individual. I always knew who had schizophrenia. It was so obvious. Mentally I imagined how it would have felt to make the picture, and I would imagine the world through the eyes of the artist. If the drawing was full of condemnation, burning up, persecution, things flying apart—if it felt familiar—then my guess was they had schizophrenia. I listened to the "visual language." If I understood the words, then I figured it was from a familiar land. I was more skilled at this than anyone else in the class.

I wasn't taking my medication because I couldn't study and think clearly enough when I was on it. I loved doing the free drawings every day. I was drawing all throughout the day when I wasn't in class. At night I walked for hours out along the back roads, passing through the dark, steep forest.

I wasn't getting much sleep.

The day came for me to start my art therapy internship at the Vermont State Hospital in Waterbury. I rode in a car with several other students who would be working as interns there, too. When we arrived, I saw the big walnut and maple trees and ancient, red-brick buildings that were more than a hundred years old.

We went to the main building, past the reception area, and I saw my first patient. He was an older man, bent over at the waist and moving his arms and legs like they were out of his control. He moved in a strange rhythm—to his own desperate song. He could hardly walk; his arms and legs were going in spasms. His tongue was going in and out of his mouth, vulgar and quite fast.

It looked like a worm, going in and out of a hole.

Like a scared worm that could not make up its mind.

He seemed to have no control over any of this.

We were walking toward him. We regarded him, and he saw us. I didn't want to look at him, really, yet he was a spectacle that I was drawn to watch in a voyeuristic way.

But I looked down.

Our guide said, "Hi, Jim." Jim grunted back.

We walked past him and continued down the hall.

I felt shaky. I felt sick.

I knew that what I had just seen was a person with tardive dyskinesia, which is a side effect caused by taking antipsychotic drugs like the drugs I was taking. I had always heard about this condition and worried I might get it someday, but I had never known how it looked. Panic raced through me. I had a terrible feeling in my gut. I wanted to get out of there.

The sight of Jim replayed over and over in my mind.

It wouldn't stop.

Over and over the desperate worm went in and out. In and out.

The hospital was miles of nineteenth-century halls and underground tunnels, all old and depressing.

I met the patients who would be in my art therapy group. The group I was in charge of leading consisted of women with severe mental illness, mostly schizophrenia, on a locked ward. I visited the ward and saw their sad little rooms. It was strange to be visiting a hospital in the role of a therapist and not as a patient. On the day of my first group at the State Hospital, I tried to dress in a professional manner so I would look like a therapist, not a patient.

I was playing a role. It was a strange feeling. I felt like an imposter. I was a little scared I would be found out. I didn't want to blow my cover. I didn't want anyone to know that I too had been diagnosed with schizophrenia. It was my secret. I was going to stay "in the closet" because there didn't seem to be any other way. If anyone knew my secret everything would fall apart. I would be shunned.

I got to the ward. The group of women had gathered at two long tables. I came bearing precious art supplies: oil pastels, chalks, paper, colored pencils.

I got to know the women each by name. I was nervous but comfortable with them at the same time. I gave them the supplies, and they started to draw. This old hospital was a place in dire need of art, even though the color and life of the drawings did not really fit in. The dark weariness of the place actually seemed to beg for some gesture of life—even a small gesture—a chalk picture of a clutch of flowers or a pencil drawing of a beloved pet cat. These expressions brought forth a bit of a spark of the life force—the same life force that was so easily deleted from the hearts and minds of the patients. Some of the women had trouble getting started, and I tried to encourage them in the process. We made small talk. They seemed glad to be doing something different from their daily routine. They shared their work with one another. A few women kept their work hidden and to themselves. Some were proud of their efforts. One woman started to cry.

"Did your drawing make feelings come up?" I softly asked.

She nodded tearfully.

"Do you want to talk about it?"

No, no, no.

"That's OK then. It's all good."

She calmed down.

The group finished up, and the women took their drawings. Some would be hung on bare white walls. Some would be saved and given as gifts to visitors. Some would be hidden away.

"We're so glad you came," they said to me. "We're so glad."

It was night. I was back in the woods. The voices were screaming at me:

"You must be punished!

"You must kill yourself!

"Bad, Bad, Bad!"

There was an old stone wall. I pounded it with my fists until there was blood. I needed to feel the sensation of pain. The sensation of pain in my hand eased the pain in my mind.

The voices went on and on.

Everything was a blur.

In the morning I awoke in a hospital in Burlington, Vermont. I didn't know how I got there. My arms and legs were strapped to the bed by leather restraints. I had never had this done before.

I needed to pee. The aide put me on a bedpan.

Shame. Humiliation.

Necessity.

I went in and out of consciousness. I didn't know how long I had been there or what had happened.

At some point they removed the restraints and said I could get up. I tried to stand up, but I was too dizzy. I couldn't do it.

It was a medication side effect.

I had to be pushed around in a wheelchair for two days because they had me on so much medication that I couldn't walk.

After a few days I returned to Goddard College. It was a new week, and I went back to the State Hospital to lead another drawing group with the ladies on the ward. I was glad to see them, and they were glad to see me. I liked them, and it was a productive group. We were now more comfortable with each other.

There were many drawings and good camaraderie.

But later that night the voices went after me. I ran out through the forest. Things were flying apart inside of me.

"You must die!"

I could not endure this.

I walked and walked and walked into the night, for hours in the deep blackness.

The voices were subsiding as I got back to my dorm room. The dark night started to gradually fade to day.

Finally, it was morning.

On my untouched bed in my room there was a message waiting for me. It said I was to go to the school health clinic at 10:00 a.m. There was no explanation. I walked across campus with some curiosity and much apprehension. When I got there, they immediately took me into an examination room.

There was the doctor.

And there was Gladys, the art therapy program director.

And there were several other people.

Gladys spoke:

"You must leave Goddard College and go into the hospital. You can no longer be in the art therapy program."

(I noticed that one person went over to the window and blocked it and someone else blocked the door.)

"If you do not go into the hospital voluntarily, you will be committed to the State Hospital. If you go in voluntarily, there is a general hospital that will take you in Barre.

"It's up to you."

She wasn't mean about it. I could tell this was very hard for her. She was just stating the facts. We were friends. It had just come down to this; this was my situation. I had caused this, and I knew it. I had just been thrown out of the program.

I was thinking fast.

I didn't want to be a patient in the place where I had just been a therapist. I would go voluntarily to the other hospital. Things were matter of fact. I didn't try to argue.

Outside, a woman in a car was waiting to take me directly to the hospital in Barre. Gladys hugged me. I got in the car and left Goddard College, and it seemed like forever—that I would never return.

The drive was long. The voices were condemning me.

I didn't know the woman who was driving.

The staff at the hospital seemed to be expecting me. Straight to the Emergency Department. The nurse took my clothes and put me in a hospital gown. I was told to sit in a wheelchair and was pushed into the elevator, then upstairs to a room. There was a female patient in the bed closest to the window with the curtain drawn. I had to get into the bed nearest the door.

The noise in my head was roaring.

A woman in white was saying something to me, but I could not understand her. The side rails of the bed went up.

The voices and the noise intensified.

I struck out with my arms against the side rails of the bed.

I needed to feel some boundaries so that I could tell where the edges of my body were.

I was fighting against the voices.

I was fighting them with everything I had.

They were howling.

People came in and took my hands and ankles.

They tightly tied them with pieces of cloth to the frame of the bed so that I could not move.

I struggled even harder.

I was aware of someone giving me an injection.

But the struggle went on and on.

Gradually, I started to wear down a little.

I went into darkness.

I had no concept of time.

After a long time, I became aware of a woman sitting in a chair by my bed. I had no idea how long she had been there, or how long I had been struggling.

"Who are you?"

"I'm Sister Kathryn."

"Sister? Are you, like, a nun?"

"Yes."

"Why are you here?"

"I do this when it is needed." That was our entire conversation. There was nothing more to say.

Still, I was glad that she was there. She sat next to me, demanding nothing, saying nothing.

It made a difference to have her there and to not be alone.

She held my hand. My other hand had an IV. My hand started to swell up and hurt.

The nurse came in. She looked at my swollen hand, and she got angry. "You've pulled the line out! We'll have to start it over!" She was genuinely annoyed with me.

They gave me more shots. More pills.

They told me my stepfather was on his way to get me and take me back to Texas.

I didn't want to go back to Texas, but I was relieved that it was my stepfather and not my mother who was coming to get me. He was always so calm and rational. Much better than my mother, who was overly emotional. He would not be too excitable about all of this. There would not be too much drama.

I was lying in bed. Sister Kathryn was gone. I was alone, except for the lady in the other bed hidden behind the curtain. I thought I had been there several days now, but I wasn't exactly sure.

I started wiggling in the restraints. I kept working on them, and one hand started to get loose.

Looser, looser.

I nearly had it free now.

One hand was free!

Now I was working feverishly fast.

The other hand was easy!

I yanked the IV out of my hand. A sting of pain, but I didn't care.

Two free hands! Next the feet.

No one was around. No one could see me.

I freed one foot, then the other one. I jumped up out of bed. I was shaky. Was this OK?

I decided it was OK enough.

I had to get out of there. This was my chance.

I left the room and saw an EXIT sign nearby. It was a stairwell. I went through the door and descended, very fast.

Down, down, down.

The door at the bottom opened. I went down a hall. No one was there.

I saw another door. I went through it—suddenly I was outside!

Bright cold air slapped my face, but the sun was warm, and the blue sky was dazzling!

I ran across the parking lot.

There was a field with tall grass and brambles. The brambles tore at my bare feet and legs.

The gown didn't want to stay on. I struggled to stay upright. I didn't know where I was going, but I felt like I had better run as fast as I could.

Suddenly, there was a man dressed in a white in front of me. I tried to turn away. He reached out and grabbed my arms tight. I struggled but didn't say anything.

"You're going back!" he said sternly.

The gown kept coming open, exposing me. I tried to close it.

He held my arms tightly and pushed me back across the parking lot into the building.

With him holding onto me tightly, we went up the elevator, then back to my room.

This time they didn't try to put the restraints back on me. But I didn't try to leave again, either. It was obviously useless to try to get away.

Now it was morning. The nurse informed me that I was to be discharged. There was going to be a meeting at 10:10 with a social worker and my mother.

My *mother?*

She wasn't supposed to come!

It was supposed to be my stepfather! My heart sank.

I couldn't bear to see the effect of all of this on my mother. She always took things so hard. It kills her, and I hated to watch. Once when I was in high school, she got a call at work that I had been found unconscious in the gymnasium after I had overdosed on some anti-anxiety pills. Her response was that she fainted. She simply could not bear it. I hated that I did this to her. I knew this was going to affect her hard, and I didn't want to see it.

At the meeting, the social worker told us it was "*imperative*" that I go into residential treatment. She repeated this over and over in various ways to make sure my mother and I understood.

A residential treatment facility.

A necessity.

A must-have.

Do this.

Go there.

You must.

You'll be there a long time.

My mother and I survived the meeting. We finally left the hospital and went to dinner at a fancy restaurant. It was a vast contrast. We spent the night in a plush hotel. I was so glad to be out of the hospital.

The next day, we drove back to Goddard in the rental car and packed up my things in boxes. My mother had arranged to ship my things.

I said goodbye to a few classmates. I had not lasted in the program for even a whole term, but I still had become connected to a few of the other students. We hugged each other and were all are in tears.

On the flight back to Texas, I looked out the window. I felt like a real failure. I didn't want to go back to San Antonio. I didn't like that my mother had to bring me home. Again, I felt like such a failure, and I hated this feeling.

I've got to do something with my life, I told myself.
But right then, everything seemed nearly impossible.

Impossible.

I had failed again. This was the unavoidable theme of my life.

I was a failure. Over and over.

Failure.

Failure.

Failure.

"Untitled (No. 21)"
Charcoal, pastel on paper
80 x 100 in.

FOUR

She painted animal forms on the walls of her
cave...and slowly, as the blood paint dried,
the animals began to slowly move a little bit,
as they came alive...this is the magic, this is the
creation of real art, art that is not quiet, that
will not stand still—and it is the
ultimate reality she told me, as my
eyes adjusted to the dark.

Portland, 2018

Isn't spring supposed to be the time of renewal or rebirth? It is the first day of April—and both April Fool's Day and Easter, all at once. Is that a bad joke? I'm not too sentimental about holidays. But it is the last few hours of the weekend—and I am sorry and sentimental about the weekend being nearly over.

I have spent the day repairing the paper edges of my enormous drawings, "The Human Beings." They will be shown next Thursday at the gala for work. I drew them years ago, in pen and ink on the biggest paper I could find. I had not known that paper came in such big rolls, but when I saw it, I was thrilled and knew what to do. Unfortunately, that paper was not too sturdy, so here today, years after drawing them, they are looking a bit fragile and ratty. I carefully mix wheat paste with torn pieces of Japanese rice paper to make the patches. This is the correct technique to repair art on paper. I'm glad to have this knowledge.

I had a discussion this week with my 93-year-old mother, who told me that I should never have drawn them on paper and that I should sell them to anyone who wants them. Get rid of them, since they are delicate. (What if we got rid of people just because they're not sturdy?) For her it wasn't that I should sell them for a good price, or to a place where they will be seen by more people—it was to just sell them to anyone in order to get rid of them. She and I have gotten into so many uncomfortable conversations about my art where she tells me that I should not put time into drawing on paper because it isn't as valuable as work on canvas. She doesn't seem to understand that sometimes a subject calls to be drawn on paper, and not to be painted. When making art, it's important to be led by the subject or image one intends to portray. One must use both one's eyes and hands, but also one's heart and soul. And probably even one's senses of smell and hearing are part of the process, too. Making art requires all of the artist, and even more. My mother tells me that I should only paint landscapes because they will sell. And she doesn't like any painting unless it is very realistic—in art language, the term is *representational*. Sometimes the ephemeral quality of drawings is just part of their truth. And landscapes don't tend to be very brave. We go around and around on this. She prefers the paintings I did when I was first learning to use paint on canvas, because they are safe, familiar pictures of subjects that she understands and finds pleasing: landscapes and still lifes. Pretty and not confrontational. No emotion. She doesn't think that anyone would want to buy my more difficult, expressive works—they are difficult because I paint them from a mind state of edgy emotions. She sure doesn't want to see them.

I was recently surprised when my mother actually said that she liked an oil painting of mine that unexpectedly sold for thousands of dollars last January. The painting is of a person whose head and body are just a loose cluster of black lines, who is clumsily holding a bouquet of flowers. The painting is titled "The Gift." I painted it after a long hard winter when I had been very depressed and my husband, Kent, presented me with a bunch of yellow mums and blue bachelor buttons. It's not exactly a happy painting, but it does have flowers. I wonder if she would still like it if it had not sold for such a surprisingly high price. Probably not.

I don't try to make pretty art, just honest art. I think that if a painting is honest, then it will likely be beautiful, even though looking at it may not be easy. Beauty is sometimes hard. Being beautiful and being pretty are often miles apart. Can't we say the same thing about people?

For me, making art is about communication, and I value communication that is genuine. So many things I can't say, except for through my drawings and paintings. Sometimes, I need the immediacy of drawing on paper because that is the best, most honest way to communicate something. Sometimes, oil paint and canvas are needed instead. If I didn't have this way to communicate then I would probably combust. Doing this is as essential as eating and sleeping.

I remember once when I was sharing the drawings in my portfolio with a neighbor. I laid them out in a long line on the pavement of his driveway. My neighbor had a friend visiting—a very quiet, older man. As he looked at the drawings, one by one, he began to cry. My neighbor whispered that the man's wife had recently died. He had recognized the pain in my drawings as his own.

I have been thinking about a quotation I read recently: "Art is the highest form of hope." It was said by the German artist Gerhard Richter. I wish I could have a conversation with him. How did he live—was the hope of art enough? What made him need to find hope in making art—what was hard, but most importantly did creating art really help? Beauty helps me have hope—at least sometimes. (Note the lack of decisiveness.) Is beauty essential? Maybe at times art needs to be ugly, because it needs to tell about some injustice, or pain. But even this sort of ugliness will have a sense of beauty because of its honesty. Is it true that truth is beauty, and beauty is truth?

This starts to turn into a philosophical exercise, and I stop it because it can smash away all the energy and emotion that pushes an image to be created. It's good to ask questions that sometimes drift into the realm of philosophy, but if the art gets too stuck inside one's head—the rational mind—then the juice and energy of the piece of art can be sucked away, and the spark of creation just disappears.

I was pondering what I need to stay alive on the planet. The answer I came up with is that I need to be able to paint and write. Doing these things helps my life have a sense of meaning. When Mother and Ananda are gone, I will still be able to paint and write. At least some. Perhaps my life will continue, possibly for a little while. The thought of the end is not far from my mind. Today, on this rainy Sunday afternoon I am longing, just a little bit, to be more hopeful. And then I look around me, at the rapturous beauty of early spring, and the sound of the rain, and suddenly the thought of ending my life seems like a sad and unnecessary idea.

Not everything is glum. At the work gala next week, Ananda will be wearing her new "little black dress" made just for her out of black velvet with rhinestones. I am not the sort of dog owner who insists on dressing up my dog. Ananda detests wearing clothes, even her service dog jacket, so I rarely make her wear anything except her collar. We both compromise when she is performing her official duty of service dog and she wears a purple vest that says "Service Dog—Access Required." This vest is her ticket into restaurants, stores, my office, and airplanes.

As I contemplate thoughts of my dog wearing her new fancy coat, and how the rain is nurturing the soil, and how art persists beyond the small lives from which it emerges, I feel more hopeful.

And I am grateful, too.

San Antonio, 1978

I was determined to go forward with my life—no one was going to tell me it was impossible—but I was becoming well acquainted with a pitch-black world where I could only beg for the end.

I was back in San Antonio. I knew the social worker in Vermont had said I should go to a residential treatment program.

Oh yes, I knew.

But I didn't want to hear about it. Surely her words did not apply to me.

I decided I would get a job.

I was going to work with emotionally disturbed little ten-year-old boys in a treatment center for kids with psychiatric problems. I figured I was qualified to do this since I had a degree in psychology, plus I had been in art therapy school—even though it was very brief.

I moved into a little studio apartment next door to my boyfriend, Peter, who had a small cottage on a converted dude ranch on the edge of the city. There were still open grassy fields around the ranch, but on the distant edge there were the inevitable acres of identical new tract homes with the dismal, heartless architecture that I abhorred. In the San Antonio of the past, cowboys—or "cowfolk"—used to live at "dude ranches," but it had become repetitive miles of bland, soulless neighborhoods.

Peter was in his first year of medical school. We had started dating when we were undergraduates. He had a canoe, and we would go on camping trips on the green waters of the rivers that flowed through the unpopulated "hill country" north of San Antonio.

We had grown very close—we were in love, even. One night, after months of dating, we were in a small park in the suburb near my parents' house. Peter got very quiet and serious all of the sudden, and stood before me, with a solemn look on his face. He took my hands in his, our eyes met, and he said, "I want you to be the mother of my children. I want you to be my wife. Will you marry me?"

I was shocked. I knew we loved each other and had grown very close, but the thought of getting married seemed way out of anything I had been imagining for myself, or for the two of us. And being the mother of his children?—I didn't even know if I wanted to ever be a mother. The thought of having children was frankly very frightening.

This was shocking and really scary. It was impossible. After a very long silence, I told him that I loved him, but I couldn't say yes. I didn't really understand why I couldn't, but I wasn't ready to be married, even though I loved him. He listened quietly and didn't seem totally surprised by my answer. He didn't seem surprised, angry, or upset. Finally, we embraced and then walked in silence, hand in hand, back to the car.

It was my first day of work at the children's treatment center. I was responsible, along with a man named Carlos, to arrive at 5:45 a.m. and start the day, rise-and-shine, for a dozen upset little human beings who were very unhappy with the world and their predicament. Carlos skillfully cooked them handmade tortillas and eggs scrambled with potatoes, while I roused them from their slumber. I softly called them by name and lightly touched their feet through the blankets. Some were quiet and subdued; others roared and cussed like drunken sailors. Most of them were on medication, just like I was. Carlos and I had to dispense it to them. I was struck by how strange it was for me to be passing out medication to anyone—since I loathed taking it so much myself. Of course, this was my secret. I felt like a cruel hypocrite. Some of them took it without much of a fuss, but a few of them didn't want to go along with the plan, and it got to be a Big Deal. I understood them not wanting to take it because I didn't want to take it either, and the harsh irony of me dispensing it to them was profound. But this was my job. I had to do it.

Most mornings they had school. A special teacher would come, and everyone would go into the classroom. In one of the first classes I attended a boy named Stevie got very upset and agitated and was told to take a time-out. I was supposed to monitor him. I escorted him to the Time-out Room, and he was furious. He turned around and started furiously hitting me and spitting into my face. My face felt the warm, wet liquid. I was amazed. This was a new experience. I tried to hold onto his active little arms, but they were pummeling me quite fast. I had never dealt with anything like this before. I tried to put my arms around him, to hold him and calm him down, but that didn't work. I backed away, and we were both crying. He stopped fighting, and we both just stood there, looking at each other, with tears running down our faces. Standing there, staring at each other, crying together and trying to catch our breaths, we were stuck together in this awful, timeless scene. After that, he didn't hit me anymore. Time-out was over. I escorted him back to the classroom.

Another little boy named Cody was always bullied because he was overweight, and the other boys thought he was a sissy. My heart went out to him. I tried to be his friend without it being obvious.

There was another little boy named Eddie who had it in for me and would attack me with his fists whenever he got the chance. I didn't know why he was so angry at me, but when I went to wake him up in the morning, he got up swinging. There was a very small boy named Harold who always tried to protect me from Eddie. Harold was much smaller than Eddie, yet he risked his life and limb to come to my defense. I didn't really understand why he did this—I certainly didn't expect it. But he was very brave, and his gallantry touched me. He reminded me of a human Mighty Mouse: small, but strong and heroic.

I had been working at the children's treatment center for just over two weeks. The only thing I could do with the boys that seemed to help was to draw them pictures. They would watch and tell me what they wanted in their own personal drawings. I drew whatever they asked for: monsters, castles, all kinds of animals, race cars, and rocket ships.

On this day, the nagging voices in my head were loud. The boys had eventually gotten bored with my drawings. My internal voices were becoming impossible, too loud for me to do practically anything. I had been struggling with them all day. No one at work knew this was going on in my head. I surely didn't let anyone in on my secret.

At the end of the workday I was finally able to go home. The voices in my head had combined with the energy of the anger and fear of the little boys. I had absorbed the profound suffering of these children all day long, and I didn't know what to do with all the pain and trauma. The result was a massive feeling of sadness and fear inside me. I was completely drained from trying to hold it all in.

The phone rang. It was my Aunt Leah, my father's sister. He had gone to live with her in Shreveport, Louisiana, after my parents divorced and he got fired from his job at the airline.

"Why don't you ever write your father?" Aunt Leah demanded.

(Accusation.)

"He haunts the mailbox, waiting to hear from you."

(Guilt.)

"You're letting him down."

(Bad Daughter.

Bad Child.)

I started to sink.

Deep.

Deep.

Deeper.

Down farther.

There was too much pain. I had let my father down.

Too much pain. I couldn't save the little boys at the children's hospital.

I could not do this. I could not go on.

The voices yelled at me: Kill yourself! You must die!

It was the only answer.

I always knew it would come to this.

The voices were howling now.

A Death Chant.

I went in to the bathroom.

To the medicine cabinet.

So many bottles of pills. All different shapes, colors.

So many. So many.

I opened the containers and held them in my hand. There were more than three handfuls.

I took them.

I took. I took. They choked in my throat, but I forced them down.

I didn't have to wait long.

Darkness.

I wasn't sure where I was. It was a strange place.

I wasn't sure what happened, how I got there.

I went back to sleep.

Awake again. A woman in white.

"What happened?" I asked her. "Where am I?"

"This is Northeast Hospital. You nearly died, but your boyfriend found you in time. Lucky about that boyfriend of yours."

But I didn't feel lucky. I felt like a hideous, broken creature.

Everything was so confusing; I didn't remember much. I slid back out of consciousness.

For the next several days I went in and out of sleep.

I didn't know about anything around me, and I only vaguely remembered the overdose. I didn't think much about my deed.

My mother and stepfather came to visit. I didn't want to see them, especially my mother. She looked terrible, her eyes all swollen and red. I knew I had done this to her.

"Leave me alone! I can't stand seeing you right now!"

It hurt too much to see what I had done.

It made me want to die all that much more.

I didn't deserve to be alive. I poisoned everything.

I was grateful when the nurse came and gave me another shot.

The dense, groggy feeling filled my head and silenced my guilt for a little while.

Sleep was the only blessing.

The effects of the overdose had worn off. Peter had come to visit me. He wordlessly stood by my bed and silently looked down at me, his arms by his sides. He wasn't smiling. There was a very long, hard silence.

Then he sternly said:

"I'm very disappointed in you."

I said nothing. I had disappointed the one man who loved me.

I laid there. I understood his words. There was no escaping them.

I had let him down.

I had let the whole world down.

Yes, I understood, and I had no defense.

And that is all there was.

I was in a meeting with my mother, stepfather, and the social worker of the hospital.

The theme being discussed was that I needed long-term residential care. This was the exact same topic that had been discussed with the social worker in the hospital in Vermont. This time the idea would not be ignored, denied, or discounted. The social worker recommended two hospitals. One was Timberlawn, in Dallas; the other was Austen Riggs, in Massachusetts. They had the best reputations.

I wanted to know if I would have to take medication at these hospitals; I didn't want to take medication.

Yes, medication was part of the treatment program in most places.

Then I didn't want to go. I didn't want to be stuck someplace and be forced to take a lot of drugs that were going to make me feel bad.

"You have no choice."

"You have no choice."

I had no choice.

I managed to make a phone call to Harry, a therapist I had seen once before. He was very unconventional, which was why I kind of liked him. And I even trusted him a little bit. He said something intriguing that I wanted to hear: "There is this place in California. They don't give you drugs. It's a very different kind of place. It's controversial, but no medication. And they can cure schizophrenia."

All I heard was:

No medication. And they could cure me!

The name of this place was the Cathexis Institute. It was in Oakland, California. Right next to Berkeley and across the Bay from San Francisco. Hmmm…That would be an excellent place to be. If it didn't work out, I could go north to the Cascade Mountains, or all the way up to the wilderness in Canada. And I had heard of some Buddhist groups out in California. I'd like to check them out.

I was already plotting my escape route, just in case.

Phone calls were made, arrangements were taken care of, and I had an appointment to be interviewed at the Cathexis Institute on the day after Thanksgiving. They wouldn't say if they would take me. I would have to meet with them and be there for several days, and then they would make up their minds. My mother and stepfather made arrangements to fly out there with me for the interview process.

I needed to say goodbye to Peter. I had tried to call him on the phone at his parents' house in Dallas. I spoke to his mother. I had met Peter's parents once before when he and I were still undergraduates at Trinity University in San Antonio. Peter and I and his parents and my parents all had gone out to dinner together for a happy celebration of our upcoming graduation. It had been very cordial and warm among us all. Now, when I talked to his mother on the phone, right after getting out of the hospital, I told her about Peter proposing marriage to me. She apparently didn't know about it. She didn't say anything and cut the phone call short.

A week later, when I was getting ready to go to California to see about the new treatment program, I went to see Peter at his cottage at the dude ranch where I had also lived before my suicide attempt. His parents were there visiting him.

When I arrived, we all stood out in the parking lot. I greeted Peter with a stiff hug and a kiss and then greeted his parents. They just stood there, but said nothing, and then, without a word, they turned away and looked in a completely different direction. They would not look at me. It was like they refused to acknowledge me in any way. I said hello again, but they continued looking away, saying nothing. They refused to say a single word to me. It was suddenly very clear that I no longer existed to them. They wanted me to disappear. They had found out about my mental illness and wanted nothing to do with me. They didn't say a single word or look at me, not even once. They didn't want their son to have anything to do with this madwoman. They certainly didn't want their son to marry this crazy woman; they didn't want mental illness in their family. I was to be shunned. They would not acknowledge me in any way. Peter stood there in the middle of it all, looking uncomfortable. It was obvious I should leave, so I did. Inside I was shaken. I had never been treated like this before. But I understood it and realized that the prejudice and discrimination because of my mental illness was now an overt part of my life.

THE VOICES WERE WHISPERING TO ME.

They were telling me I was bad. They whispered that I needed to die.

You must be punished.

I took my medication, and the voices didn't get too loud.

But they didn't let me alone, either.

San Francisco-Oakland, California, 1978

I didn't have the faintest clue about what was about to consume me. There was no way I could have known—it was unimaginable.

The day after Thanksgiving finally arrived. It was the day of beginning my new life in California.

The plane touched down in San Francisco. As we drove in the rental car to the hotel, I stared out the window at the unusual vegetation. Orange birds of paradise. Blue umbrella plants. It seemed so exotic and lush compared to Texas. In the restaurant at the hotel, the waiter smelled like coconuts.

It was the morning of my first visit and interview at the Cathexis Institute. I dressed in a wool camel-colored blazer and matching wool skirt with boots. I wanted to look good. I wanted to look "professional" and competent. I felt like I was going to a professional job interview and needed to impress them. It was much better in my mind to look professional than like a mental patient.

The three of us went together to the interview.

I had my guitar with me. I thought that the best way I could explain myself to them was by singing a few songs that I had written. The song about the stars coming out at night. The song about swimming with the orca whales.

We arrived at a large, modern, two-story house in a residential neighborhood near downtown Oakland. A youngish woman wearing false eyelashes and smeared black eyeliner met us at the door.

"I am Jean," she said. "I'll be doing the interview this morning. Then, in the afternoon, you will observe the drop-in program."

She then basically told my parents to get lost.

I thought she would ask me lots of questions, but she did all the talking. She didn't want to know anything about me. But she wanted to make sure that I understood all their rules.

Rules, rules, rules.

"Can you agree to follow these rules?"

One of the rules was that I would have absolutely no contact with any of my family, except through letters. No phone calls or visits.

Another rule was that I would live in a board and care home, which was sort of like a halfway house, but more restrictive. I wouldn't be able to have my car or drive.

And I must do everything they told me to do. All those rules had to be followed exactly. They would act as my parents—it was called "reparenting," and I would be their obedient child and get reprogrammed. She said that schizophrenia was caused by faulty parenting. She said my problems were due to my mother not nursing me correctly when I was a very small infant.

My guitar sat silently at my feet throughout this exchange. I started to wish it would magically disappear. Jean ignored it.

Later in the day it was time for what they called Daily Drop-In, when all the patients and staff got together in the main room, the large living room, and I was there to observe it. I sat on one of four long sofas arranged around the walls of the room. Young adults, about twenty-five of them, both men and women, started to come in and take their seats. Some sat on the sofas, but others sat in front of them on the floor. Some of the ones on the floor were getting their shoulders massaged by the person behind them. There was quiet talking, but the atmosphere was quite tense. The patients weren't called patients—they were called "students," like we were just another class at the university. Most of them looked like ordinary people, but some of them looked like patients in any psychiatric hospital. One woman with red hair was strikingly skinny. Another was mumbling to herself. But most looked like they could be in any college physics class.

Suddenly, the staff came in. There were four of them—two men and two women.

Silence immediately.

There was a really big man who was the psychiatrist, Donald K. He made some announcements, and then it was time for DPS, which I found out meant "daily problem-solving" group. I went to a little room where there were about seven students and one staff. The therapist was a middle-aged woman with curly hair named Velma. Every student quickly wrote a goal with a marker on a whiteboard on the wall and then took a seat on big brightly colored pillows scattered about the floor. I tried to make myself invisible in a corner.

A young man announced that he wanted to work.

Was he saying he wants a job?

No, he wanted to talk about a problem.

He looked like he couldn't be more than eighteen or nineteen. He started telling about his problem with his roommates, and he was getting very excited as he was speaking.

Velma interrupted him. "You're getting manic, Scotty. Watch your energy." He immediately became more subdued.

The group went on and on, and everyone was taking turns talking about their problems.

Suddenly everyone started focusing on the one young skinny woman. She seemed to be in a lot of trouble for something, but I wasn't sure what. Everyone started raising their voices, telling her that they didn't like her malicious and intransigent behavior and that she had better cut it out. I had no idea what she had done wrong. Had she broken a rule? She was just sitting there, looking down at the floor, looking frozen and scared, but saying nothing. Finally, she blurted out a breathless "I'm sorry" to the group and said she would do better. The angry mob let up. Finally, the group was over. I could not wait to get out of that room.

The next group I went to was called Regression Group, and I was to observe students doing "regressive work." In this group, the students abandoned their adult functions and became like babies or young children while the staff took care of them—reparenting them—as if they were their parents. Kind of like a day care center for adults.

It was a large room filled with all kinds of toys and big, soft pillows. There were five students/patients and three staff members. Two students announced that they planned to "be" babies, one planned to "be" a two-year-old, one planned to "be" a six-year-old, and one planned to "be" a twelve-year-old. Donald K. was leading the group, along with Velma and one other therapist.

"Cathect Child!" Donald K. loudly sang out.

Suddenly everything turned upside down. Now there were two adult students wearing baby diapers. They were lying across the laps of the staff members. One was crying and sounded just like an infant. Velma started giving the adult "baby" in her lap a bottle: a Coke bottle with an oversized nipple filled with warm milk. The "two-year-old" adult student started running around gathering up toys and throwing them against the wall. Donald K. told him to stop.

"NO!" the two-year-old shouted defiantly. Velma told him that if he didn't behave properly, he would have to stand in the corner.

The six-year-old was building something with blocks. The adult student who was supposed to be twelve was having an earnest conversation with one of the staff members who was also holding an adult "baby." One female grown-up baby got her diaper changed by Donald K. Her private sexual parts were totally exposed. I watched carefully. I was shocked, dismayed, and fascinated, all at the same time. This was something I had never seen before. This was something totally different from any hospital—or any other place. But more than anything, I just wanted to get out of there.

Although this seemed very strange and frightening to me, everyone else acted like it was completely normal. The two-year-old adult male student was made to stand in the corner because he wouldn't stop throwing his toys. He quickly agreed to do what staff wanted and was allowed to play again.

I couldn't wait for this group to be over. Adults in diapers and "children" standing in the corner was too much for one afternoon.

And then Donald K. loudly sang out, "Cathect Adult!"

Just as suddenly as it had started, everyone acted all grown up again. Those who were acting like babies just a moment ago were now rubbing their eyes and smiling.

I could hardly breathe. I got up and bolted out the door. The program was over for the day.

I was free to go. I rushed out of there.

My mother and stepfather were waiting in the rental car in front of the house.

How was it? How do you like it? They were too eager.

"Well, it's not like the hospital," I told them. There wasn't much else I could say. How could I tell them what I had seen? Would anyone believe it unless they had seen it for themselves?

The next day, we visited the board and care home where I would live if I were accepted into the program. It was a dreary, depressing one-story house in a criminally active neighborhood. Multicolored graffiti covered the tall cement wall that surrounded it. The emotionless residents, men and women of various ages, were sitting in the bleakly darkened living room on stained chairs with stained carpet and blankly staring at the blaring TV, chain smoking cigarettes. I realized that it would be a very long bus ride from there to the institute.

My parents and I all looked at the sorry scene. None of the residents seemed to notice us. No one spoke. The television blared with static.

We went back to the hotel to wait for the call to see if I was accepted into the Cathexis Program. The call came. My stepfather answered.

He gave me the news:

"You're staying."

I'm staying.

I'm staying.

What did this mean?

Oh, shit.

All I could think to keep myself from sinking down is that I wouldn't have to take medication anymore. And there would always be the Cascade Mountains to the north. And this was where they can cure schizophrenia.

This is why I had come.

This was why I was here.

OK. I'm going to do this.

Somehow.

I would have to remember why I was there.

They cure schizophrenia here!

This was the only place I could get well and not have to take medication.

I would do whatever it took.

Whatever it took.

My mind was made up.

Whatever it took.

I would do it.

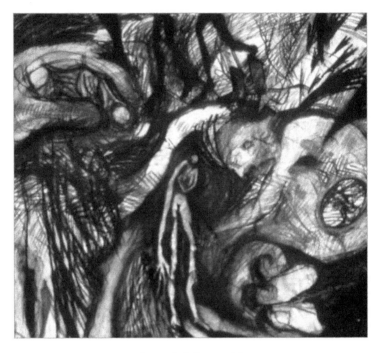

"Untitled (No. 19)"
Charcoal, pastel, on paper
52 x 90 in.

FIVE

Have the roses all finished their display,
have the hydrangeas abandoned their seasonal
sprint, and you, where are you in your life, has
your blossom been spent, is your bloom a thing
of the past, is your season pulling its way to
a close, or is the gestational urge coalescing
deeply in your bones—she asked me this, while
pulling on her boots (for the first time since
last spring)—oh it's not like that at all, she
remarked, and laughed, and out the door
she flung herself, out into the pitch
black late summer night.

Portland, 2018

Today is the warmest day so far this year; the sky is blue, tulips of every color are blooming, parents are pushing their progeny in strollers, and it as if the world has come back to life after being stricken by catatonia. The sheer beauty of it all—the colors, the light, the sensation of the breeze on my skin, and how even the shadows are finally allowed to play and gracefully dance upon the ground—it rouses my senses, despite my inward gaze.

I just took Ananda for her walk amidst all the beauty, and what occupied my thoughts? Yes, I did see the gloriousness; yes, I did appreciate the breeze; so why was I thinking about the possibility of going to Switzerland for doctor-assisted suicide? I read that they do this in Switzerland and some other countries for those who don't have a terminal illness, but who have depression or bipolar disorder. And maybe schizophrenia?

Am I not grateful enough? Is my heart without love? I ask myself these questions over and over, but there are no answers in the songs of the birds that call brightly from tree to tree. Instead, I tug impatiently at Ananda's leash and hurry her when she tries to sniff a bush for more than a moment.

I feel like a monster who doesn't belong in this mild scene.

Yesterday was the birthday party for Ananda. I filled the house with all shades of pink tulips and rosy camellia blossoms. The chocolate cake said "Ananda = Joy" in white butter icing. Ananda's name means "joy" or "bliss" in Sanskrit. It is the perfect name for her, and it is perfect for me to have a dog with this name.

Was this all a charade, a lie, a ruse?

Ananda's many admirers came, some bearing gifts of dog treats, toys, and a pink bandana that said "Love" for her to wear around her neck.

One of the guests, Beth, told me that she loves Ananda, and then she pointedly added that she loves me, too.

Kent came late in the afternoon, near the end of the event. Ananda was extra happy to see him, jumping for joy—even though he finds her barking more taxing than he can tolerate. I think she regards him as being her father. All three of us, together, make a pack. Not a family, but a pack.

I had not planned to eat any cake; I'm trying again, for the hundredth time, to stop eating sugar. But I ate a piece of the buttery cake anyway. Was it a happy time? Was it worthwhile? Do I regret the occasion?

I'm really not sure of the answers to these questions.

Today it is like a bad hangover. Is it the sugar? Why is this foul state enveloping me? Am I supremely ungrateful and turned inward in a narcissism usually reserved for certain politicians? And about the politicians—currently that is a whole other subject that is a reason for despair. Or maybe anger, on top of the despair. No, this isn't about the state of our nation or the economy, it's not about global warming, and it's not about the poor polar bears and hundreds of other creatures who are losing their habitats due to the destructive habits of us humans.

No, this is something else, like a scaffolding encircling my heart so that it cannot beat with the warm rhythm of life.

OK Meghan, snap out of it. Stop it. Stop the ingratitude. Stop feeling sorry for yourself. Stop feeling sorry for anything that you are making up in your moldy mind.

Tomorrow is Monday; the weekend is nearly over. And although the sun still sits above the horizon, I think I best take my medication, pull the blinds closed, and go to bed. On days like today, I must remind myself that I am OK in the most profound sense. I must remind myself that I have full-time employment that would be impossible if I were still overwhelmed by so many hallucinations. I'm well now, right?

Sometimes when it is like this, it reminds me of the old days when my world was such a fearsome place, when the only predictable aspect was the psychic pain. But mostly it is different now.

Remember, Meghan, remember! Things are different now! You're all right! It's all OK.

Sometimes one can only fold it all up and pull the covers over one's head and hope that the night will come and obscure all of the supremely unhelpful thoughts.

OK.

Sometimes it has to be enough just to submit and hope that sleep will be the deliverer of relief.

Good night, good night.

Oh, good night, chrissakes!

Oakland, 1979

Where in the world was I now?

The world of the Cathexis Institute was a world unto itself. I had been in Oakland for a couple of months. I was living in the depressing board and care home, and every day I rode the city bus for two hours to get to the afternoon Cathexis drop-in program. I had learned how to dress and behave in ways that didn't draw attention to myself on the bus. I blended in. I didn't want trouble. It was an accomplishment to get through the ride without being hassled by someone. The seats of the buses were covered with graffiti, as were many of the buildings in the neighborhoods we rode through.

Head down. Keep to myself. These were my mottoes.

I arrived at Cathexis a few minutes before 2:00 p.m., the appointed time. Other students were waiting out on the porch. We were not allowed through the door until exactly 2:00 p.m.

When the doors opened, we went in and started finding seats. Everyone seemed to be somewhat tense. There was a little talking in quiet tones.

The staff came in, and the meeting started. Silence. The staff was unhappy with an issue in the "community"—the word that referred to us students. The students were being confronted about something that I didn't understand. One male student, a man in his late twenties, started to argue with Donald K.

Other staff members joined in the argument. The volume was growing. Mark, the young man, was getting angry and upset. Everyone else was now quiet. There was shouting.

All at once, Mark leaped to his feet and started toward the door.

As he moved, ten other people, both staff members and students, jumped up as if activated by springs. They surrounded him, and in a moment's time he was on the ground, everyone wrestling with him, on top of him.

"I've got a leg!"

"Do you have his head?"

"I've got his head!"

"I've got his right arm!"

"I've got his left leg!"

He was entirely under control, restrained on the floor by these people who rode the movements of his thrashing body like a rodeo calf. It happened so fast that I just sat there, stunned.

He slowed down his movements.

"Let's take him to the corner!" shouted Donald K.

With the choreography of a dance troupe, they carried Mark to the corner of the room.

He was placed face to the wall and restrained by two of the brawnier men with his arms held up high behind his back in a way that looked like it must hurt. Whenever he tried to fight or resist, they raised his arms higher.

I was shaken by the violence of this display but also impressed by the efficiency with which the intervention was carried out. I felt scared. While Mark was restrained in the corner, big pillows were placed over the windows to muffle any noise that might alarm the neighbors.

A "community meeting" of students and staff was held to make a plan for Mark's supervision while he was punished in the corner. I got the feeling that this was going to possibly go on for hours and hours.

Mark was making noise, trying to yell and cuss at the people holding his arms. Someone put a cloth gag on him, and then he was only able to make small, muffled noises through the gag.

I went to a small group in another room, and we talked about our feelings about Mark.

It's the best way, everyone said. But some of us said that it was a little scary, too.

I learned that I would get training in restraint techniques and be expected to help restrain anybody who needed it, just like Mark. Anyone who breaks the rules can expect to end up like this. It was the way they did things here.

I didn't have to stay and help with Mark because I was a new "kid"—they always called us called "kids" or students. They never called us "patients." I stayed for a while and saw that after a very long time Mark was allowed to use the bathroom under heavy supervision. I was told that he would be given a can of liquid food supplement to drink as nourishment.

The next day, the corner was empty. I learned that Mark

had apologized and repented the error of his misdeeds to the satisfaction of the staff after seventeen hours of standing in the corner. I hoped that would never happen to me. I decided I was going to be very, very careful not to make anyone angry.

I would have to be perfect, so I would never break a rule.

The Cathexis Program was started by a woman named Jacqui Lee Schiff and her husband; they "reparented" a young man with schizophrenia and apparently cured him entirely of his disease. She went on to do this with other young people who had schizophrenia and then taught the technique to other therapists. It is controversial, I am told. I am told that drug companies want to undermine the work since it does not rely on using medication. I am told that one criticism is that it is considered to be "brainwashing," but that I should disregard this because it is not true. I must relearn faulty beliefs that have come from my natural parents, especially my mother. I am told that Jacqui Schiff expects to receive the Nobel Prize for her pioneering work.

I wasn't told that the year before I had arrived a young sixteen-year-old "kid" with paranoid schizophrenia had broken a rule and then been hog-tied and put into a bathtub of scalding water. He died from his burns. A reparented student who had been in charge of him was charged with manslaughter, but the charges were eventually dropped. No one talked about this. It was unimaginable, and I didn't have a clue.

I didn't find out about it until years after I had run away.

The Cathexis explanation is that schizophrenia is due to problems that arise from incorrect parenting, especially, in my case, from the way I was incorrectly breastfed in the first three months of life. They had a particular diagnosis for my type of schizophrenia: they called it hebephrenia, which was a word that is based on the Greek child-god, Hebe. The goddess Hebe was thought to be able to restore youth. Hebephrenia was associated with problems at a very young age. I learned that it was the worst possible thing a person can be. Again, I was sentenced to a terrible predicament. I hated this label. Hebephrenics were supposed to be the sickest and have the most terrible form of schizophrenia. We were supposed to be malicious, dangerous, immune to pain; everybody had better watch out for us, we're so bad. We do deplorable, awful things to people, so therapists and people have to protect themselves against us at all times.

According to the strict rules, I had to tell about an impulse I had to hurt myself. I had accidentally bit the inside of my lip when eating a peanut butter sandwich. It really shouldn't have been a Big Deal, but I was scared to leave out even the most mundane little detail.

While I was talking in the group, the therapist was giving a baby bottle of warm milk to another student, who was curled up across the therapist's lap. The student cried like a baby, then in went the milk. I was already accustomed to seeing this kind of scene. It happened in just about every group, sometimes several times. Other students asked each other or a staff member to "hold them," and they were held across the lap, in the arms, like oversized babies. Students who were not being held asked each other for "strokes," which consisted of shoulder massages. This was a very physical place. But it wasn't all sweet and lovey-dovey.

I had to confess to staff about every little thing, every little time I felt like hurting myself.

Staff demanded that we tell them everything, the truth, at all times. My confession about the peanut butter sandwich went over like a bombshell. It was more severe than I ever could have imagined. I was going to have to talk about it that night in treatment group. I had to make a contract with the therapist not to "act out" until then.

My treatment group of six "kids" and two therapists met once a week, every week. It was the group that determined the goals and content of my treatment at Cathexis.

I was very nervous. I had to talk about my self-destructive impulses. At this point, I was off medication, and I felt like a volcano about to erupt. I had to sit there and do everything right, act perfectly "normal." I had to say the right things. Be perfect. The noise in my head was so loud.

But I had to behave appropriately. It was expected. The consequences of messing up would be dire.

"I want to work," squeaked out of my mouth.

OK.

I told them that I'd had impulses to hurt myself, and I had accidentally bit the inside of my lip. I was sorry. Very sorry.

They asked me some questions. Was I going to do anything else to hurt myself? What was my plan to control my behavior?

I wasn't sure what my plan was, except not to do it.

I learned about a thing called a *procedure*. In a procedure, you made a contract to "go into the craziness" and, with protection, you got into the crazy state. People kept you from physically hurting yourself by physically restraining you. You would explore what is behind the craziness or do whatever it is you need to do in order to resolve the issue while in this psychotic state. It lasts until you have done whatever it is that you "need to do." The craziness takes over, and you give yourself to it in an environment that is considered safe. The goal is to resolve something that needs solving but cannot be done through rational means. One of the therapists asked me if I wanted to do this.

I thought about it.

I did.

I made the required contract, and the procedure was scheduled for the day after next.

I was nervous.

I had all of this energy and noise and voices going on inside me that I was working so hard to keep the lid on. What was going to happen when the lid came off?

It was Wednesday. The day of my procedure.

The time was 1:00 p.m. I was in a large room. The windows had all been covered with big brightly colored pillows, to block out any noise that I might make. We couldn't let the middle-class neighborhood's residents find out about what we were doing. All furniture had been removed from the room.

Twelve students and two therapists had assembled. I was wearing jeans, a T-shirt, and socks. I was told to stand in the middle of the room. Everyone formed a circle around me. There was a strong feeling of tension and expectation. No one talked. Everyone was just watching me.

"Is everyone ready?" asked Donald K.

Everyone said yes.

Then he said to me, "Do what you need to do."

I silently stood there.

I felt something building up inside me.

It was the howling of the voices; it was the rage, suddenly it was like I was on fire—

I was flying through the air; it was all coming out—

There was movement, struggle; I was fighting, fighting. My inner voices were screaming at me.

I was scarcely aware that people had caught hold of me and had deftly brought me to the floor. They were securely restraining me there. I fought as hard as I could.

I saw faces of insects and devils and bright flashes of colors.

I continued to fight with my arms and legs and everything I had. Sometimes I felt like I was tangled up in a web.

The voices went on and on, condemning me, howling, screaming.

I yelled back at them and fought them. It went on and on.

The people were holding me down tight, like a cowboy in a rodeo riding a wild bull.

When it got a little quieter, Donald K. asked, "Who are you talking to?"

"It wants to kill me!" I yelled.

"You can tell it to go away," he replied.

Leave me alone!

Leave me alone!

I want to live!

The struggle went back and forth. The voices condemned louder.

I yelled back at them: I want to live!

I WANT TO LIVE!

The noise in my head started to grow weaker. Something was happening. I wasn't fighting the people holding me down; I was fighting the voices. The people kept a tight grip, all the same. Eventually the voices started retreating like a shabby rodent, retreating to its hole, after being chased by a fierce terrier. I was lying there on the carpet, my chest rising and falling, out of breath.

The room grew quiet for the first time in a long while. Just the sound of my heavy breathing.

"How are you doing?" Donald K asked finally.

There was a long pause. "OK, I think."

"Do you still need to be restrained?"

I thought hard about this. Were the voices just lurking on the edge, ready to rush back in?

"No, I'm OK to be let go. Thanks, you guys."

And I was struck by how amazing it was that I just went through all of this and nobody came and shot me up with an injection of Thorazine, like so many times in the hospital. And nobody had tied me down. This was what is different about this place.

Slowly I got up, and everybody hugged me and said, "Good work."

I went home for that night with three girl students who lived in a nearby apartment. I wasn't supposed to be left by myself so soon after a procedure. That night I lay on the floor in a sleeping bag at the girls' apartment. I thought about the day, about the procedure. It meant a great deal to me to not be in the hospital after what I had heard and seen that day. The fact that I wasn't given Thorazine or a shot of some other drug meant a lot to me.

And now, I wasn't by myself.

I wasn't alone.

I just became a true believer in Cathexis. After this experience, I thoroughly dedicated myself to the program. I wanted to get well. I could do it here, only here.

I was working with Dyanne, a woman therapist with whom I felt a secure connection. Dyanne was middle-aged, with olive skin and short curly black hair. She liked to dress in flashy clothes and high heels, and she wore lots of eye makeup, green eye shadow. She was very nurturing, although she also delighted in saying things that were shocking, just to stir things up.

I called her on the phone every night to say good night.

I was in a group where Dyanne was going to give me a bottle. I was lying in her arms, across her lap. Her body was ample and warm, very soft. I felt safe there. When the time was right, I started to cry out.

It was a baby cry; I didn't know how I knew to do this; it just came out.

I felt young like an infant, totally vulnerable.

Something was on my lips, something warm and soft. I opened my mouth; there was milk. I sucked.

All was warm.

All was safe.

I was filled.

This woman.

This milk.

I sucked until I was full.

I basked in the feeling of fullness and safety.

"Cathect Adult," she finally said. This meant we all were again expected to act like grown-ups. The group was over. I went back to my regular adult self.

I decided to move from the board and care home into a house with three other women students. We all had different diagnoses of different types of schizophrenia, but we wanted to live together away from board and care. We rented a house in the suburbs of Oakland. We still had a long bus ride to and from the institute, but the living situation was going to be more agreeable. I got to know the women, my new housemates, more closely. One woman, Brenda, was doing very intensive work with a therapist with whom she had a parenting contract. That meant that she called him "Dad" and considered him to be her father. His day job, when he wasn't a therapist, was in advertising. She often stayed overnight at his house to do "intensive work." Another therapist, who was only a senior in high school, was also usually involved. The work, as I understood it, had to do with "stimulation issues" and "masochism." I wasn't exactly sure.

I passed her in the hall coming out of the bathroom. She wasn't entirely dressed. I saw her legs, up to her underwear. Her legs were totally covered with gigantic purple bruises, as I had never seen before. They entirely covered her whole legs. I was shocked.

"Brenda! What happened to you!?"

"It's the work I'm doing with my Dad," she replied nonchalantly.

I couldn't believe that anyone was inflicting those bruises on her on purpose. I did believe her, but it was so incomprehensible.

She told me that she couldn't go to a regular doctor because the bruises would cause so much suspicion and be bad for Cathexis. But she said Donald K., the psychiatrist, had checked them out and she was OK.

A warning bell went off in my head.

This was not right!

This was wrong. Nobody should do that to another person, in the name of therapy or whatever—it was not right.

I needed this place to get well.

This was the only place I could get well.

They can cure me of schizophrenia here.

But where in the world was I?

Was this OK?

Could I stay here?

I was at Dyanne's condominium. She had me over nearly every week now. Four other students were also there.

It was night.

I was in Dyanne's king-size bed, lying right next to Dyanne.

My arms were bound up with pieces of cloth webbing, so I couldn't move them.

She gave me a bottle of milk. Lying on the other side of her was another student. Another student was in a sleeping bag on the floor. Two more "kids" were in other bedrooms.

My hands were so securely bound up in the nylon webbing that it served as a restraint, just like when I was restrained in the hospital. So were my feet. I had to be bound up like this because I was a hebephrenic and therefore very dangerous.

I could barely move.

The lights were turned out, and I tried to go to sleep.

I was aware of Dyanne's body next to mine.

I couldn't sleep.

I lay there.

I heard voices.

The night went on forever. I listened to all the breathing going on in the room, and soft snoring.

Finally, at 6:00 a.m. I was relieved to hear the clock radio blast on: time to get up. Then back to Cathexis.

In restraint class, we learned the techniques of how to restrain people.

You've got to be ready to do this at all times.

This gets drilled into us, over and over.

Be ready. Be ready, be ready.

Never wait—always jump into action.

I learned all the different positions. I practiced them. I learned to be vigilant.

Don't relax for a minute!

You can't let down your guard.

No one was safe from getting restrained.

I had been at Cathexis several years. I walked the walk, talked the talk. And now I was going to do what was called regression work. In treatment group I made a contract to be a three-month-old baby for two days. They made arrangements.

Dyanne was going to be the primary caregiver, but there would be other people involved to help. On the first day of the regression work, she said, "OK, get little."

So, I got little. I "cathected" the mind of a three-month-old baby.

It was surprisingly easy to slip out of adult reasoning and have the mind of a baby. In my mind I was no longer an adult. I was put in a cloth diaper and a T-shirt. My mind was wide open, and I wanted Dyanne. She held me. I cried; she gave me a bottle of warm milk. There was no sense of time. At one point she fed me something sweet, some fruit with a spoon. I was just in this open, timeless state.

I had a feeling in my lower abdomen. God—I had to pee—could I do this?

But I did. My pee came out into the diaper all wet and warm, and it was a great relief.

Dyanne soon observed that my diaper was wet and wasted no time changing it. A few people helped her. I was vaguely aware of being exposed with my bare legs apart up in the air, exposing my most private anatomy; on one level I was thinking "Oh My God!" But this was just how it was, and it seemed all OK. Not a Big Deal.

I slept, I cried, I was held, I was given a bath, all naked. I got bottles. Another diaper. Moment by moment, time passed. Night. Day.

"Cathect Adult!" said Dyanne.

And immediately I became an adult again. I really don't know how to explain that I knew how to do any of this. It seemed so natural.

I felt grateful to these people who had taken care of me.

It felt strange, but I felt like I did something I needed to do to get well.

Weeks later I was at the Federal Building in San Francisco.

It was a Big Deal. I had never done anything like this before.

I was going to testify at a public hearing on mental illness. I was the second one to speak.

I got up and went to the podium. I had notes for my speech, but they were sealed in a notebook, out of reach. A thousand miles away on the lectern.

When it was time for me to begin my testimony, my mind went blank.

I said nothing.

Silence.

Everyone in the audience and the panel was looking at me, expectantly. Notes out of reach.

"I need a moment to collect my thoughts," I said finally. A long moment passed.

I figured I had to take the leap and started talking.

I began to talk about what it is like to take medication. I told about the side effects I had had. What the drugs did to my body—how I felt about the changes to my body. I told about what it meant now to not go to the hospital all the time, to find a different way to treat mental illness. I said how against medication I was and how important it was to not take medication.

That was my testimony. I went and sat down.

A man from a TV station came over to me and asked me if he could do a story for the local nightly news on me. A newspaper reporter came over and requested an interview. I was a little dazed by their attention. I was still rattled from giving the testimony, but I talked to each of them. I gave a quick interview to the newspaperman, and then went with the TV reporter and a cameraman to the San Francisco Zoo. The TV man thought the zoo would be an exciting place to shoot the story because I loved animals.

I was in the petting zoo surrounded by goats, alpacas, and lambs. The TV man asked me questions about what I thought about psychiatric treatment while I fed a very bright goat some pellets of food. The goat tried to eat my hair and the buttons on my shirt. The cameraman recorded it all on film. I tried to pet every animal in the enclosure, and I was thinking this was a great deal. The zoo people seemed to be giving us free access to wherever we wanted to go. After the petting zoo, we went by the gigantic, black gorilla in his little metal cage. I thought he looked terribly sad. Then we went to a small pen with a huge brown curly haired buffalo. I reached through the fence and petted him on his nose. It was wet and sticky.

Suddenly, I had enough.

The TV people sensed that it was time to quit, too. The adventure was over. The story was shown on that night's news broadcast.

Sometimes I got away from Oakland for a few days. My cousin Sherry and her husband, John, lived in a cabin in the Santa Cruz Mountains, south of Oakland. Sherry was ten years older than me. When we were together, she seemed more like the sister I never had than a cousin. She was fun to be with, and I loved to visit her and John. The little mountain community where they lived was a unique place, very backwoods—lots of freethinkers and nonconformists. Sherry and John owned and ran the small general store that was the hub of the community. They loved good food, wine, and friends, and were very generous to everyone, especially to me. When I visited them, I forgot about Cathexis. I felt kind of like a regular person when I was there.

I tried to tell Sherry about what it was like at Cathexis. I could tell that my description was having an emotional impact on her. She seemed shocked by my stories of regressive work and people being spanked. But she didn't say too much and offered no judgment. She asked a few questions. She told me that if I ever needed a place to stay that I was welcome in her home. That seemed a little odd to me, but I put it in the back of my mind.

Back in Oakland I had become a runner. Every day, I went for long runs in the hills above Oakland. Sometimes twelve or fifteen miles. My body had become quite thin. I was strong and lean since I no longer had the side effects of the medication. I was happy about this; it felt good to me. This was the way I wanted to be.

Of course, I still had the voices, but I was expected to function correctly, and there was tremendous peer pressure from the other students to behave perfectly. I couldn't look or act crazy for one second, or I would be confronted. I had learned thoroughly to act "normal." I had to be continually watching all the other students to see that they were responding appropriately, acting normal, and confront them the minute they deviated. It was extremely important that no one show any sign of being "crazy." Most of us managed to do this, at least most of the time. The consequences of not doing it would be severe. Maybe I would need to restrain someone. We all had to act perfectly normal.

Running through the hills helped me deal with all the stress of the voices and having to hold them inside me and behave correctly.

I ran and ran.

At a community meeting one day, everyone was yelling at this one girl. She had done some little misdeed, and now it was a Big Deal, and it was like a pack of dogs was upon her. I felt sorry for her, because I knew she didn't have a chance. She was told to stand in the corner. She got up and did what she was told to do. I didn't think she had a clue what the issue was that she was being confronted about. A plan was made to supervise her in the corner until she "solved the problem" and "dealt" with the community. This meant we were going to be there for hours, maybe all night. People took turns watching her, and others went for pizza and sleeping bags. It was a kind of party atmosphere.

I hated it.

I saw her body growing unsteady on her feet as the time passed. She asked "to deal," but when she tried to speak her ideas were rejected. She said she couldn't stand there in the corner any longer. It had been hours now. Two people got behind her and pulled her arms up behind her back, forcing her upright, onto her toes. They held her like this. I knew it had to be killing her.

I wanted it to stop.

But I didn't dare say a word.

I watched. And waited for it to be over. She said she had to go to the bathroom. Four people took her. Then back to the corner. Hands up behind her.

Eventually, it was six in the morning. It had been many hours. She was exhausted. She apologized and said she understood how she affected the community and would never do the bad thing again.

They finally released her.

Later that day, at afternoon drop-in meeting, we were all gathered waiting for the program to begin when Donald K. made an announcement.

The girl who had been restrained in the corner was no longer in the Cathexis program. She would no longer be here.

She decided not to stay.

We don't discuss her.

We moved on to other business.

But I was stunned.

She left!
She's free!
I was happy for her.
And a little envious.

Later that week I was told that as part of my treatment I would now have to go to something called "The Game." The Game was held in a large room and consisted of about fifteen students and two therapists. The only rule was that you must stay seated in your chair the whole time that The Game was going on.

It was my first time in The Game.

I was scared.

I was in my chair. The Game started.

The way it worked was people started to verbally assault one another. The rule was that everyone can say anything, and you try to say the most horrible thing you can think of to someone in order to upset them. It didn't need to be true—just cruel. The cruelest verbal assault. You were doing really well in The Game if you were saying the most terrible, upsetting things to someone and it was getting to them and tearing them down. The goal was for people to get their defenses torn down. For people to verbally hurt each other. Pure verbal violence. It got nasty fast. People insulted each other about their most personal and vulnerable things.

The energy in the room rose up, and then the other participants ganged up on one man about his sexuality. Apparently, he was gay. When he started to cry the focus moved on to the next victim. I was scared stiff. I tried to insult a therapist about his smoking habit so that no one would focus on me. I was just trying to survive. I didn't escape for long.

One person turned to me.

"So, you're working with Dyanne, huh? You'll never have a parenting contract with her!" Someone else chimed in, "Hebephrenics don't ever get well here—you're fooling yourself!"

"Dyanne can't stand you. Don't you know that?"

"You're a hopeless case!"

"Poor Meghan—such a hopeless case!!!"

Hopeless case—hopeless case!

And it went on and on and on. Crueler and crueler. Just enough of it true to shake me down deep.

I kept telling myself to stay in my chair, I've got to stay in my chair. Stay in my chair. Stay in my chair. I reached down and tightly gripped the plastic seat under me. I grabbed it tight so I could focus on something substantial. The attack by other participants continued, relentless.

But it was true what they were saying. The voices in my head started to accompany the voices of people in the room.

Everyone was yelling at me.

You're no good!

You're unlovable!

You're bad! Bad! Bad!

You must die!

"I'm staying in my chair!" I screamed back at them.

It was all I could do, just stay in my chair, but I was falling apart. I desperately squeezed the arms of the chair so that I could tell where it was. Everything else went out of focus.

The noise was exploding my brain.

"Stop The Game!" Donald K. suddenly ordered loudly.

Immediately everything went silent.

I was still tightly squeezing the arms of my chair.

"We're removing you from The Game," Donald K. sternly said to me. He got up and took me out of my chair, out of that room, to a group in another room. He told the therapist of the group that I had to be removed from The Game, and I should be held.

I felt huge relief to be out of The Game, but the voices were still screaming at me.

The therapist of the group held me in their lap, but my adrenaline was still coursing through my body, and I felt like running and running far away.

It was a few days after The Game.

During community announcements, Donald K. said Dyanne was not working at Cathexis anymore. And then he nonchalantly moved on to making other announcements.

She is gone!

Just like that!

I can't believe it!

How can this be true?

He was very vague about the reason. Something about differences in leadership style, or something—I didn't know—I had stopped listening. All I heard was that she was gone.

I depended on her—how could she not be there?

I could not get well without her.

Shock.

Sick feeling.

Sinking. Sinking. Sinking.

There went my reason for being there.

There went my reason for enduring everything that I encountered to be there.

How could I possibly get well if she was gone?

A few days later, a new therapist came to take Dyanne's place. I talked to her briefly. She was young and earnest.

I couldn't care less.

All that mattered was that Dyanne was gone.

Life was without pleasure.

I was getting nowhere.

I was not getting well.

Why was I here?

I had been here for four years of my life now.

I felt like I had accomplished nothing.

It had been good to be off medication and not go to the hospital—but at such a cost! And I just couldn't keep explaining away the atrocities anymore. The students were getting physically punished, violently treated. I knew it was wrong.

I had enough.

It was time to leave.

I called Sherry to see if I could stay with her and John. Her answer was an immediate "Yes!"

At the community meeting, I tried to announce to people that I had decided to leave and tell them why. I wanted to tell them goodbye. But the staff were confronting all of the students—the "community"—about some other unrelated issue, so I wasn't getting a chance to talk. I just watched the poor students squirm and say anything to try to get off the hook and placate the staff.

I thought to myself: I'm so glad I don't have to play this charade any longer!

I knew that Sherry was waiting for me outside in her van. I couldn't put off leaving any longer. I couldn't wait for this confrontation to be over. I had to go.

I got up and walked to the door and left.

It was that simple.

I went through the door, and out to the van with Sherry. "I'm free!" I said.

"You sure are!" Sherry replied.

We drove home to her cabin in the mountains.

I called my mother from the cabin. "I left the program, Mom. I'm at Sherry and John's."

She was cautiously overjoyed.

After so much time, there was much to talk about. Since we had not talked in over four years, it was awkward at first, but it was good.

That night I went to bed in the attic room of the cabin. My first night free.

I could not comprehend that I actually had left the program.

I could not understand what it had meant to be at Cathexis and how it had changed me. The trauma of the experience had scarred me deeply.

It was nearly unthinkable that I had actually left. But I knew it had left its mark on me and I would never be the same person.

I was so glad to be lying in that bed, far, far away from all of the people and rules and practices that had governed my life. I snuggled down deep into the covers and felt the warmth. I listened to the night sounds. I heard an owl hooting deep in the darkness.

I was ready for whatever would come next.

"Mother and Child"
Pen and ink on paper
30 x 40 in.

SIX

Each word she spoke contained a blue storm,
there were only the arguments of children who
spoke in sentences of redemption;
the night held all blue secrets and the servants
of the clouds clustered together and looked
down upon the earth—they are looking now,
and her voice still calls out true.

Portland, 2019

I wrote to the owner of the gallery today and said that I wanted to take back my painting "Blue Cello, Yellow Dog." It has been in the gallery for over two years now, and even though we have lowered the price, it has not sold. At a recent work fundraiser, a young woman I had never seen before came up to me, totally unexpected, and said that she had seen the painting there and that she loves it. I figure I would probably buy the painting myself if I had not painted it. I have faith in this painting, and it has two of my favorite things: 1) dogs, and 2) cellos.

Sometimes making art is such a lonely thing. One does what one must, to be honest and have integrity, to not "sell out." Maybe when I am a no longer living artist, after I have died a tragic death, maybe then there will be commercial interest in my work. One can only hope. Hope, and keep making art.

Would I rather be a happily living artist without financial success, than a tragic, miserable, dead, but valued artist? And maybe it is possible, since my paintings lately are brighter and more upbeat than for many years. Maybe it really is true that art is the greatest form of hope!!!

I will just have to keep on being true to the images that insist to be drawn or painted.

Tomorrow morning at eight, I am going to be interviewed on a live radio show. The reason is that tomorrow is the first day of May, which is "Mental Health Awareness Month," and since I have bona fide schizophrenia, they must have thought I would be an appropriate guest. Actually, as I think about it, I remember that it was all in response to the press release about me winning the suicide essay contest. Ahhhem—I mean, winning second prize.

I hope that I can get by just talking about art. It is much more interesting talking about art than talking about mental illness. Or politics.

Even though I now work in the field of mental health, I am much more interested in making art than I am in being a poster child for recovery.

There, I said it.

Mental illness is intriguing if it is in the abstract or at a reasonable distance. I used to try to convince myself and others that being mad was a romantic experience. Of course, I don't mean romantic as in love; I mean that I argued that it was a lofty, noble way to live. Tragedy in and of itself was worthwhile. And then you die, of course.

There are journalists who can write an exciting story about mental illness, even though they don't have a real clue or firsthand knowledge of the actual experience of having a psychiatric condition. I know of a famous and well-respected journalist who makes his living writing critiques of people who give and receive treatment for serious mental health conditions. He mainly critiques the use of medication, but I doubt he's ever taken it or needed it himself. He is even considered an "expert" and is a hero to people who agree with his opinions. I met him one time and wondered how it is that he is so renowned when he doesn't know firsthand about his subject. And I felt judged by him because he thought I was "less than"—a subpar schizophrenic—since I take medication for my symptoms. I felt like I needed to defend myself from him. And he didn't have a clue of my own history of activism against the use of psychiatric medication. He assumes it's a simple issue and people like me are weak and have sold out. According to him, I shouldn't take medication, but just suck it up. The people who have been diagnosed with schizophrenia but don't take medication are somehow better, more independent than those of us who use it.

This is really not helpful.

Tomorrow morning, at the radio station, I will have to behave myself and not be rude. I need to be aware of the anger I still have, but not just blast it out. I will be honest, though. I will not be rude, but I will not make things up to say just because it will help people feel cozy and warm about an otherwise tough topic. I hope that maybe I can say something like "I would rather talk about art," and that the interviewer will say, "Sure," and then off we go. I might be able to get away with it since I can quote the German artist, Gerhard Richter, and say, "Art is the highest form of hope." Isn't surviving serious mental illness or psychiatric illness essentially everything about hope when it comes down to the dreary nuts and bolts of it all? And if art is the highest form of hope, then—there you have it, ladies and gentlemen—the topic should be art.

Not dreary sickness.

Not today.

Not tomorrow at 8 a.m.

So, I have got to navigate my entire way through this month, well-meaning as it is, and somehow find a way to make it all about art, not threadbare and relentless disease.

OK, this is my assignment. This will be my challenge. Maybe I can even turn it into my little secret mission: to change the topic to one that I want—the importance of art-making. I think that maybe I will be able to explain that years ago when I stopped defining myself as "Meghan the Schizophrenic" and just embodied "Meghan the Artist," my life got much better. OK, in all honesty, I am not making my living by my art. Instead, I make my living by having survived, at least so far, a dreaded illness and sharing the story over and over with people who want and need to hear it. And using my experiences to design mental health programs that are better than what I have experienced in much of my life.

It is like walking through fire. I can do it, but I'm not too sure I can tell you how to do it. But maybe just the fact that I can do it will be enough to cheer you up. Or give you—what's that word?—hope!!!

Today in my painting studio I worked on a painting of

another Winged Being of the Sky. Winged Beings are benevolent beings whom the everyday rational mind cannot believe or see. But they are everywhere! The sky is full of them. This is certainly an unusual thought for most people in the Western world, but in Tibet, for the Buddhists, this is accepted as a regular, unchallenged thought.

Ever since I discovered the Winged Beings, I have been seeing evidence of them everywhere. I see evidence of them in the wind as it blows through the leaves of the trees, in the little seed pods that are everywhere in the fall, in the raindrops in the Oregon sky—I could go on and on.

Of course, I know this might sound like hallucinations. If I told you about electricity, or gravity, or DNA, and you had never heard of them before, they also might sound like hallucinations.

I had an appointment with my psychiatrist recently. I realized that I had better not bring up the Winged Beings subject with her, because she might have thought I had relapsed, but at the last moment I felt the need to share this amazing discovery. I took a deep breath and then explained to her about the Winged Beings and their paintings I am working on right now.

She didn't tell me I am crazy. She basically said that there are many common beliefs in our culture that are stranger. I was so pleased that she didn't give me grief about the subject. Actually, in my eyes, her credibility and skill as a doctor increased. But I won't try to convince the average "normal" person.

I would rather paint Winged Beings than watch television. Watching television is a widespread activity in our culture. Does anyone watching the football game stop and question its validity?

I won't try to convince anyone to look into the sky and sense the energy that resides there.

My friends are all tolerant of my beliefs, even when the beliefs are unusual. My friends are just happy because I am not thinking about suicide. If my beliefs help me find a way to be a human being and live on this planet, then hooray!

Some people with schizophrenia entirely don't believe they have it—there's even a medical word for it: anosognosia. But most of us who have been given the terrible news that we have a horrible disease believe it, and that's when life stops.

We expect the worst. Everyone expects the worst for us. Everything we see and hear confirms the worst. The worst, on top of the worst. And then more of the worst. Tomorrow on the radio I will talk to anyone listening who has been given a diagnosis. I will say, just give it up—not that it will go away or be any less valid, but your diagnosis will lose its grip on your life, and once you no longer define your experience with this label, then you can start to live a new, happier life. It's not that everything immediately changes, but things will start to look a little different, and you may start to see some new opportunities. When you're walking down the sidewalk, you will see that twenty-dollar bill just lying there. Maybe you'll be like me and hear about a treatment opportunity that is marvelous. Maybe you will take a risk and start a conversation with the person behind you in the grocery store checkout line. It won't be a conversation about mental illness—no, it will be about the virtues of a fine cheese, say a Gruyere, and if the cost of organic mangoes is worth it. It will just be the most normal thing in the world.

Actually, for many of us who have been given labels like schizophrenia and bipolar disorder, the word "normal" is anathema. "Normal" is considered boring and flat. I'm certainly not saying we should deny mental illness, or emotional pain, but we shouldn't let it suck out all of our life juice. When I was first diagnosed, there were years of arguing with my doctors about did I have it or not. I always said no, I didn't; and they always said yes, I did. Finally, one day, their arguments won me over, and I "accepted" that I did have this terrible disease. I saw myself as "sick." I bought into the label. It's not that I was happy when I was living in denial—far from it.

But when I accepted my diagnosis of schizophrenia, I also lost all hope.

And my life got very small and threadbare.

There was a long time that it was so small and constricted that I didn't want to live. Who wants to live a life that is small and pathetic?

I tried and tried to end it—yes, the overdoses, the emergency rooms, the drama of being brought back from death's door, over and over. But finally, I got in touch with that little kernel of—what was it?—a spark of the life force. I had that keen but tiny little spark buried deep inside me, and once I brought it up for a whisper of air, it caught fire and burst my life open—then I realized that I did want to live after all! And the more air I gave it, the stronger it got. Finally, it was a roaring blaze, and at that point, it took over the small, sad life. I realized that I was not made to be a sick, little, constricted soul. Instead, my reason for being, the raisón d'etre, is to make art, to love dogs, cellos, birds, and waterfalls—to embrace my life! Of course, it's hardly that simple, and it is still not a pleasant, smooth straight line. Sometimes it is hard to be in touch with this will to live. But the overall direction has changed.

So, tomorrow morning I will go to the radio station and talk to that one person who is listening who needs to hear this story.

Santa Cruz Mountains, 1983

Suddenly I could breathe—there was air—I gulped it into my starved lungs.

I had escaped from the terrible and bizarre Cathexis treatment program in Oakland and had come to stay with my cousin Sherry and her husband, John. They lived in a small cabin in a little community called Redwood Estates, deep in the Santa Cruz Mountains, just west of Los Gatos.

When I was in Oakland, I would occasionally journey over the bridge to San Francisco to visit the art museum. One time when I was there, I beheld some remarkable drawings on pieces of paper that were bigger than any paper I had ever seen. I didn't know drawing paper existed so big.

Later, I was very excited when I was in an art store and found, for sale, a roll of paper that was giant—as big as the paper I had seen in the art museum. This was what I had been looking for, actually craving.

Now it was time to start drawing.

I unrolled the huge paper roll and cut off a piece about three feet wide and six feet long, then laid it down across my cousin's dining room floor. This piece of paper was bigger than a person.

I started to draw, in pen and ink, with my special pen called a Rapidiograph. The tip where the ink came out was as small as a sewing needle.

Tiny lines. Huge space to fill.

I took my time.

I had to lie on my belly across the paper, with a thick wool fisherman's sweater under me, padding my body so I didn't damage the paper. The ink wouldn't flow out of the pen if the paper was upright. My hand moved slowly, in sure, smooth, controlled motions, skating across the surface of the paper.

My pace picked up, and the energy became intense. My hand knew where to go, even though I had no plan of what I was going to draw. Soon, it was as if I were dancing with the thin black and white lines. This was the same kind of drawing I had done when I was doing free drawings in art therapy school. I let my hand move wherever it wanted to go, with no conscious control.

The dance went on and on, and time ceased to exist.

Gradually, I became vaguely aware that the image of a human figure was emerging on the paper. It was as if someone was appearing in my lines on the paper in the patterns of dark and light. I stopped drawing and carefully stood up, so I didn't damage the precious paper.

When I stepped back and looked down, I saw that I had drawn the beginnings of a male human being.

Who is this?

Why has he come to me to be drawn? I didn't know.

It was as if he had insisted that I draw him.

And it was different than anything else I had ever drawn before. I was surprised to see this human being regarding me from the white surface of the paper.

I asked myself again: Who is this?

I did not know the answers to my questions.

I got back down on the floor and continued to draw, now with a renewed sense of urgency. I sensed that this drawing was the beginning of something important. I continued to draw all through the night. Finally, it was getting light, and I stood up and looked out the big window and saw the giant redwood trees, across the canyon, lit up in the pink and gold early morning light.

I looked down at the drawing that I had been drawing for more than ten hours.

Yes, it was a human being, and suddenly, I was shocked to recognize it as a picture of my father.

I stared at it, in wonderment, for a long time. It was like he drew himself, and had reappeared in my life, after years of us being estranged.

Why had he come to me like this? What did he want from me?

Maybe he just didn't want to be forgotten.

Days went by, and I continued to draw more human beings. I never knew in advance who I would draw. It was as if these people just magically appeared from my subconscious. They insisted to be drawn, and even if I didn't want to make a specific line or shape, they overcame my will and pushed me to automatically draw them.

After four weeks at Sherry and John's house, I heard about a nearby cabin, where a young woman named Lisa lived. She was about my age, with olive skin, dramatic hazel eyes, and a long dark braid down her back—just like mine, but dark brown. She was looking for a roommate, and we immediately liked each other, so soon I moved in.

I continued to work on the big pen-and-ink drawings of people. I now called the series *The Human Beings*. I had finished three of them. I felt like they were real people, like

I knew them. I didn't know where they came from; I only knew they had demanded to be drawn.

Lisa and I began to get to know each other and became good friends. She started teaching me all kinds of useful things, like Yiddish expressions, and how to appreciate a fine cup of coffee. She would tell me a person we knew was a *mensch*, and every morning she would brew us a big pot of gourmet coffee. We started to go running together in the morning on the path by the ocean in Santa Cruz. Afterwards, we would go to the local bakery for a warm, freshly baked croissant. All of this was a new experience for me. It was a wonderful unfolding of life after the long time of constriction and unhappiness of Cathexis.

I felt a sense of pleasure that I had forgotten existed.

One evening, when I was taking a bath, she appeared in the doorway with a big, shaggy black dog. She announced that she had named him Angus, and he was going to be ours.

It was winter and we were freezing. The walls of the cabin didn't keep out the cold winter wind, so we sat on the heater vent on the floor in the hall to stay warm. For our entertainment we watched Angus, commenting on his every little move and detail. He would lick his paw or scratch a flea, and we would watch with great enthusiasm, laughing and adoring him. There was no television, no movies, no way to listen to music; there were just the two women, and a big, black dog.

This is how we passed our time through the winter, except I also continued to draw more Human Beings.

One day I heard about a man named Ricardo who lived in a cabin up the mountain with his wife and son. He was in the later stages of a terrible disease and had been brought back from the hospital so he could die at home. A call went out to the community for volunteers who would be trained to do the necessary activities to take care of him. I went to their home, and a hospice nurse showed us how to turn him, place a catheter on him, feed him, and do anything possible to ease his pain to create a peaceful passage from life for him. A hospital bed was set up in his dining room, and outside the window, chickens clucked and made noisy chicken sounds. This is what Ricardo wanted to listen to as his death drew near.

My time with him was marked by a peaceful communication. He was blind from the radiation treatments, and his frame was now just skin and bones. Even though he was blind, when I looked into his eyes, it was as if he could see me, even though his eyes couldn't see anything at all. We would gaze at each other, somehow connecting on a level that was deeper than regular vision. We could understand each other in a manner that was uncanny.

One day when I was by his side, he was having a terrible pain in his leg. I massaged his emaciated thigh; the bone was barely covered with a thin layer of wasted muscle and skin. That evening, when I was home, I started to draw a Human Being who was an emaciated male figure, who was bald, and like Ricardo, had a peaceful, soft expression. I drew his leg, and my hand moved across the paper just as I had massaged Ricardo's leg earlier that afternoon.

When Ricardo made his final passage from his earthly life, I drew a seabird lifting up and off, across the paper, out of his chest, in final peace. This had been an experience unlike any other in my life. I was profoundly moved and felt blessed by it.

But my life was hardly peaceful.

The voices had returned, and I had to see a psychiatrist who insisted I take his medication. When it didn't seem to work, he told me to meet him outside the hospital in Los Gatos.

I felt suspicious.

I didn't want to go there, but I knew I could not continue the way I was.

When the psychiatrist and I were standing in the parking lot, outside the hospital, he told me, "We're just here to visit."

But two people in white came out and took me by my arms.

Come this way, they commanded me. I knew I must go with them.

Screaming voices, a feeling of panic.

I had hoped that I would never see the inside of a psych hospital again. I felt an immense sense of failure and defeat.

They took my clothes and gave me a hospital gown, then an injection. I curled up on the bed, crying, facing the wall.

After a week, they allowed me to return home.

I went back to the cabin and continued to draw the Human Beings. Now I drew all the time. I had finished drawing eight Human Beings.

Drawing had become the most important thing to me. Making art was all I wanted to do.

It became clear to me that I must go to art school. I had to do it.

I traveled down the mountain to the valley to the university in San Jose. I signed up for a graduate level art class, but I could not officially enroll in art school because I didn't have the necessary undergraduate degree in art—my official degree was in psychology. Years earlier I had changed my major from art to psychology, hoping it would help me to understand what was happening to my brain.

On the first day of art class at the university, I knew I must somehow convince the administrators to let me enroll. I had to do it. Somehow.

I went with the roll of my eight Human Being drawings cradled in my arms, like my precious child.

This was my chance.

When it was my turn to show my work to the others in the class, I carefully unrolled them, placing all eight of them side by side wide across the floor, in the center of the classroom. There was a very long, deep silence. No one said a word.

I looked to the professor.

She looked at me.

Then, she said, "Welcome to art school. You're in."

That was all she said.

I was in!!!!

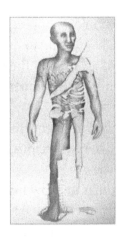

"Human Being, Male No.3"
For R.H.
Pen and ink on paper
42 x 72 in.

SEVEN

*She climbed the blue mountain with one hand
tied behind her back until the small yellow bird
freed her with its tiny beak; finally,
at the summit all unbelievers were convinced
and the stories they told their children for
all the years hence were of brave,
bright, and beautiful bodies.*

Portland, 2018

It is Halloween, which is usually my favorite holiday, but not tonight.

I usually put on my headdress with the orange and purple battery-powered lights and paint purple hieroglyphs across my cheeks. I must be careful not to make myself too scary because some of the children who come to the door are very young; they might think I'm some sort of threatening spirit, something their parents have warned them about.

But tonight, things are different. All day today, the sound of the traffic burrowed its way into my ears. I could not shut out the noise of my neighbors putting the trash barrels out. Ananda's barking at the postal carrier crossed the threshold of what I could endure. And poor Ananda, she has been sitting in front of the mail slot in the door since

9:00 a.m., devotedly waiting for the magic mail delivery of delicious catalogs and letters. She relishes biting and shaking the pieces of mail as if she has hunted and caught a juicy prey. She does this every single day, and it brings her great joy. She protects us from the wicked mail carriers—who knows what threat they will assault us with today? A dog must be ready for anything—and she always is, with a cascade of barking, barking, barking.

Anyway, tonight I cannot seem to get into the spirit of Halloween. In fact, I need to avoid it as best I can. Tonight, instead of putting on my orange and purple headdress, I will fill a cardboard box with the candy I bought weeks ago in joyful preparation. Tonight, I cannot even bear to answer the door.

I will put the cardboard box full of candy on the front porch with a pathetic little sign that says: "Happy Halloween. Take some candy."

I will turn out all the lights, so it looks like no one is home.

I can't believe it has come to this.

Tomorrow, my show will open at the gallery downtown. I should be excited and pleased. I've been working on these paintings for nearly a year. Instead of my usual monochrome of white and black, they are bright and vibrant, cadmium reds and yellows, ultramarine blue, thick pigments that speak of life-affirming emotion. Tonight, I'm asking myself if these expressions are consistent with the realities of my deepest feelings, or are they despicable lies? Have I simply chosen these pigments as a way to say, "Hey, hey, let's give a shout-out for Life"—but do I mean it? Was I telling the truth when I painted those jubilant shapes and lines? Isn't a darker, more slanted angular line, trailing off the edge of the canvas, the real truth? Can I really not endure making bright, life-affirming paintings?

Hey, Meghan, snap out of it! Stop being so morose! It's Halloween, and the neighborhood children are counting on you!

Sometimes, the truth is like this: one needs to pack it up and go to bed. One knows tomorrow morning will be a fresh day. At least one hopes.

The discarded candy wrappers will litter the sidewalk. And nothing will be lost. Next year, if it comes, it will be different, and better. Again, we will resurrect the purple and orange headdress—the frightfully painted goblin will return and answer the door yet again.

I need to give myself space and permission to retreat. It doesn't mean I have succumbed to the old dark moods. And, hey, even if I did, isn't darkness the appropriate spirit of the real Halloween anyway?

San Jose, California, 1986

Had I finally found a place in the world where I could survive?

After the first week of class in art school, my seasoned professor asked me to stay after class. This was a very unusual, curious request.

We stood together in the empty classroom, and she was careful not to invade my personal space, standing a good four feet in front of me. I think she was being careful not to make me think she was being intrusive.

She hesitated, and then launched into a speech, which she had obviously prepared for me. "Meghan, your drawings—I sense that you need a bit of support from Us."

Who was this "Us"? I wondered. What is she trying to say?

She got to her point: "If you want to make an A in my class, here is what you must do: there is a person who works at the counseling center. She is the best; you two will get along. You must meet with her weekly for counseling. You must do this if you want to pass my class."

Did I hear her correctly—was this even possible? Had she really told me I must see a counselor to pass her class?

I am in art school! How can this be happening? Is there no place where I can get away from people telling me what I need to do to save myself?

But the following Tuesday afternoon, I dutifully showed up for my first appointment with this so-called Wonder Counselor. Yes, I was feeling very sarcastic and wary. And her name? It was "Bicksey." Is that even a real name?

I sat in the waiting room, feeling rebellious and uncooperative.

After a few long minutes, this Wonder Counselor appeared in front of me. She was a whale of a woman with short-cropped gray hair, in a pale pink buttoned-down shirt. It looked like she was wearing men's trousers. She gave me an authoritative hand signal to come on, follow her.

I hesitated, but finally, with great reluctance, stood up and followed. I felt tiny as I went down the hall behind her.

Once in her office, she motioned to me to sit. I sat in the chair closest to the door. I fixed my gaze on the sky out the window as far as possible from her imposing being.

There was a long silence.

Then she finally asked, "What brings you in today?"

I continued to focus on the sky outside the window. I refused to say a word or acknowledge her question. If I must see her, to pass the class, then I would, but I certainly wasn't going to talk to her.

We sat in silence. She said nothing, and I was not about to speak to her. The silence lengthened. Not a word. Time stretched out; the minutes crept by.

How could I say anything to her? She wouldn't possibly understand the things going on in my head.

After many painful, silent minutes, my appointment was finally over. Without a word, she stood up and opened the door for me to leave. I jumped up and dashed down the hall, through the waiting room, down the stairs, out to freedom. I had survived.

One of the best things about art school was the fact that I was given a studio to work in there at the university. Actually, I shared a big room with two other students. We all had ample space and worked in our respective corners. But I had more than a corner; I had nearly half the room. This was helpful because I started working huge—massive pieces of canvas or paper nailed up on the walls.

When I was working on paintings this big—reaching nearly all the way to the ceiling—I couldn't reach the top of the canvas or paper, except by standing on a ladder or leaping up in the air, as high I as I could go, and making my mark, or brushstroke, before landing. It was like doing an acrobatic dance. One of the other women, a painter, who worked out of sight in the far corner of the studio, commented that the sound of me leaping and then smacking the paper made a rhythm, like a drum or percussive instrument. This pleased me, as the thought of making music and visual art all at once was perfect—I could not imagine anything any better than this.

I arrived at the studio in the early morning every day. For breakfast, I always had a can of Coca Cola and a Hershey bar. Perfect food for fueling creativity. There was nothing that could stop me.

Except:

The weekly session with Bicksey.

I dreaded those meetings.

Every Thursday, I would drag myself to the counseling center, up the stairs, to the waiting room, and always too soon, she would appear and summon me to her office. I sat in the same chair by the door every week. I was determined to not say a word. I would silently sit there, glaring at the sky outside the window. Bicksey would quietly sit there, just waiting for me to say something, anything. But no. I refused.

Meanwhile, things were changing in my life back at the cabin.

Lisa and Angus had moved out because she had fallen in love with a red-haired, red-bearded fellow who made her heart throb. I was happy for her because she was obviously thrilled by him, and he by her.

So, I was left in the cabin alone.

But not for too long. I heard about a woman my age, named Ava, who was looking for a place. She came over to check things out, and we liked each other at once. Ava was an unusual person, as she was the top ace banjo player in an all-girl bluegrass band. She was really amazing when she would get to picking her banjo so fast that her fingers just disappeared in a flurry. We tried jamming together, me on my cello, her on her 'jo. It was not the best fit, but we didn't care; it was all an experiment anyway, so anything that we could create was interesting.

After we had been living together awhile, Ava told me something intriguing. She said there was a fellow who was a groupie of her band who showed up at every gig, without fail. And he was always alone. Ava said he was extremely handsome and extremely shy. The thought of this person just dangled in the air. His name was Kent. I was curious but didn't think about her report beyond our conversation.

It was Saturday night, and Ava's band was going to perform at a tavern down in the valley. Ava invited me to attend. I was happy to go and take a break from school.

When I got to the tavern, I was told there was a big dilemma. The usual waitress had gone to help her friend, who had gone into premature labor. There was no one to wait tables. Ava asked me if I wouldn't mind doing it. I was horrified by the thought. But then, with trepidation, I decided I would just jump into it; I had never done anything like this before, and it would be one more adventure. A bartender showed me how to correctly pour a beer. You had to hold the glass at a certain angle, and pour very slowly, and then the foam wouldn't go all over the table. He said that I would get better tips if I at least poured some of the beer for the customers.

OK, to hell with it. I launched myself with dubious enthusiasm, and abandon, into my new role.

The night went forward with the band playing twangy love songs and music for rounding up the corral. Isn't this what bluegrass is all about? I wasn't sure, but I liked the nasally heart and emotion of it.

And then, there he was. Sitting at a table near the back. I was sure this was the man who Ava had told me about. I checked him out from the corner of my eye, and more closely when I was at a nearby table. He was cute—no, actually, he was handsome! I knew I had to meet him, but how could I even be thinking like this? This wasn't like me. But the whole night wasn't like me.

Finally, I got up my courage and went over and asked him if he would like a beer. He quietly said he would like a 7UP, please. He looked down at first, but at the last minute, he looked up and our eyes connected. His eyes were amazingly blue, and I forgot everything, until a minute later, when I recovered and snapped back to my role as waitress. I got back to work. He kept requesting more glasses of 7UP. And always said please and thank you.

Finally, the evening seemed to be winding down, and most of the heavy beer drinkers seemed to have moved on. I went back to Kent's table, and we actually started a conversation. It seemed nearly natural to sit down, but in the back of my head, I was telling myself this was way out of my comfort zone.

We started a tentative conversation about bluegrass music, and he started telling me about the history of it. He knew a lot of interesting details, like that banjos had originated in West Africa. I forgot to be so nervous, and I think he did too. Eventually, we were having a real conversation. I was surprised he was so smart and knowledgeable.

Finally, the band started to get packed up. The evening was over. I allowed myself to marvel that I had survived, and I even made $12 in tips. And I had learned how to pour a beer.

The real amazement, though, was that Kent and I had connected. I got up my courage and asked him to walk me to my car. What was I thinking?! Wasn't this right out of some corny movie? Or maybe this is what the women did all the time down South, like in Texas. Anyway, it was not my normal self who was doing this. And so, he walked me to my car. And, oh my, he was really tall. There was a long awkward pause before I found my keys and got in. He took a deep breath and asked me if he could call me. I nonchalantly said yes. I felt like I was outside my body, looking down from high in the air, watching myself in this interchange. I was a stranger to myself. I casually pulled a rumpled piece of paper out of my purse and scribbled my number.

And then with relief, but also a tiny pang of regret, I started my car and drove away.

The next morning over coffee, Ava and I replayed the night before. Every little detail. She wanted to know exactly what I had thought about Kent. I wasn't sure what I thought. I had a strange mixture of giddy excitement and disbelief that I was even feeling this way.

The weekend ended, and I went back to work on an oil painting in my studio. It was the biggest one so far; it stretched up to the high ceiling. In a mixture of deep violet and ultramarine blues, there were dogs and deer and birds all flying through the air. In one corner was a blazing citron-yellow sun, the perfect complementary color to the violet. I was totally immersed in my work, and I was excited to be working on a painting so vivid and so vast.

But then Thursday came, like all the Thursdays before, and I dragged myself to the counseling center for my weekly appointment with Bicksey. I really didn't want to see her. I was dreading it.

As usual, she appeared in the waiting room and motioned for me to follow her to her office. We went down the long hall, and she opened the door and waited for me to go in first. I tentatively took a few steps in and was astonished:

A gigantic black dog was sitting there. His enormous body filled the room. I choked but immediately reached out to pet him.

"Who is he?" I gasped to Bicksey.

"This is Vulcan. He's my Great Dane. I have his sister at home."

I stroked his short, shiny black fur and whispered his name.

"Vulcan, you're beautiful!" I said.

The Great Silence had ended.

I had forgotten not to talk.

Having Vulcan there changed everything.

"Dragon"
Sumi-e on paper
48 x 120 in.

EIGHT

She sucked the juices from the fruit,
as a hummingbird, which I assume
is her true self, at least at night
in the dark
we are anything
we desire, except maybe
ourselves,
maybe we are lost-
the darkness sucks
us up into itself,
and we are
gone.

Portland, 2018

My show in the gallery downtown has opened. On opening night, a man in his twenties walked into the gallery wearing a jaunty tweed hat and carrying a Halloween pumpkin, left over from the night before, carefully held aloft, with the word "LIFE" delicately incised in its orange flesh, and brightly lit by a candle inside. He paused in front of one of my paintings, one of the Winged Beings—the one with the body of a deer, wings, antlers, and a human face. I was curious about him. His appearance, with the hat and pumpkin, was unusual, yet he seemed very nonchalant, as if this were his usual state. We started a conversation, and he began to speak about time—geological time versus calendar time, and the months of the year compared to the minutes of a day. He emphasized his words with a pressured intensity. I realized that he was probably one of my brothers with whom I share the diagnosis of schizophrenia.

I suppose in one sense, sure, he was probably speaking from a "delusional" state, but at the same time, I understood and appreciated his thoughts and we carried on a fine conversation, meeting each other in an extraordinary, mutually understood, although perhaps psychotic realm.

"Do you know the ancient time of earth-time, beyond calendars? There is any type of minute you could conceive of; so many appointments, I am told by great ancient beings. Many minutes I am told. I'm going so much, so rare, not rare. Yes, but no. I see they are offering themselves now."

"Oh yes, definitely, thank you for bringing your wisdom to the opening tonight, all ancient beings need the calendar to be opened to bright expressions of great propensity. And I thank you for bringing your solemn pumpkin!"

"Many appointments are found in the curling time of the calendar months, all my appointments, all hours, all of them, really, they are seen here. I see them all. Of course, no linear minutes, all minutes make their appointments manifest. Red, maybe yellow. Never too linear, all multitudes of beings, I'm told. Very manifest about now."

"Truly, friend, all moments, many multitudes, all so good, all so brave!"

Our conversation thus proceeded in such a way that both he and I understood each other, but I could tell from their expressions that several patrons observing curiously from nearby were totally mystified. This conversation between us was more relevant and authentic than every other one I had that evening. The language we spoke made perfect sense, from a deeper, truer realm. We were speaking a language of deeper relevance than the "How do you dos" and "Lovely shows."

After the Pumpkin Bearer and I had conversed awhile, I noticed a white-haired man watching us from across the room. He approached us and told the young man they needed to be on their way home. I realized they must be father and son. The father had brought his son to the art opening where it was possible for him to share an oral and visual language. The son had found a place of belonging with the art and our conversation. I watched them exit the gallery and was grateful they had come.

Santa Cruz, California, 1988

Kent and I were suddenly in love. We went to all of Ava's bluegrass performances and sat across the table from each other and shared kisses. We both drank 7UPs with maraschino cherries, and we shamelessly passed the cherries back and forth to each other, mouth to mouth, in our kisses. I felt a sense of gaga, surreal happiness. This man—I had never felt this way about anyone before.

We had been dating for nearly six weeks. Most of our dates were to the various taverns in the valley where Ava's band was performing. I would spend the week at school, in my studio, but when the weekend came, I was solidly with Kent.

What was next? Wasn't it inevitable?

Kent and I had always gone our separate ways at the

end of each date. But. It was obviously time to move our relationship to the next level. Kent shared an apartment in San Jose with four other fellows. It was a true bachelors' pad. When the end of Saturday night came after Ava's performance, Kent said he didn't want me to go home, and I didn't either, so next logical move: we would go spend the night at Kent's place. I was excited, but deep down, I was terrified.

He drove us to the sprawling modern apartment complex. Suddenly, through the door, inside the hall; we just stood there; I realized there was no going back now.

Kent's small bedroom was upstairs. We entered, and as I stood inside the door, I was struck by how barren it was: a disheveled twin bed, a large portable fan, a small dresser piled high with unfolded laundry, single wooden chair, painted blue, and a large cardboard box overflowing with plastic cassette tapes. The obvious question was where we were going to sleep? The twin bed suddenly seemed gaping and immense, but at the same time, painfully narrow and impossibly small.

Oh my god, I said silently, under my breath.

Actually, this would not be my very first time to sleep with a man. I had "done it" when I was twenty-eight, just to get over the weighty crucible of my virginity. I was the only person I knew who was my age and still a virgin. I was painfully overdue. It was in San Antonio with a movie theater mogul more than thirty-five years my senior. My biggest reaction to the experience was that it hadn't hurt as much as I had thought it would; in fact, it didn't feel like anything much at all. I was mainly struck by how, after the act, he immediately sprang up out of bed, and gargled with mouthwash he had waiting on a nearby table. The primary thing was that I no longer shouldered the weighty label of virgin. It was done. Over. Finished.

But here I was with Kent, a man for whom I really cared. Things seemed immensely complicated all of a sudden. We both looked at the twin bed, then at each other. Here we were, and there was no other place to go. Without saying anything, we slowly and awkwardly fumbled off with our coats and laid them on the chair. Off came our sweaters, then we wobbled back and forth as we struggled like flamingos on one leg to remove our pants. Finally, in our underwear, we quickly found our places, side by side, like wooden boards on a rack, under the beige, pilled synthetic blanket.

Kent reached over to the fan and turned it on. Its loud whirring was like a roar. But it could not mask the silence. Once in bed, our bodies touched with electricity, and we desperately wiggled around at once aroused, but unable to find a workable position. Time seemed to stand still, but eventually, we wore ourselves out, and finally I could tell from Kent's soft snoring that he was asleep. I just lay there, carefully, with our arms and legs touching, paying meticulous attention not to move and awaken Kent.

It was the longest night of my life.

The night with Kent suddenly awoke terrible monsters in my mind.

There was a vague, unsettling sense of familiarity with it all. Behind my closed eyes I could see my father, in his pale green boxer shorts, lying across my parents' bed. He was being devoured by what I later understood were flashbacks from his time as a soldier in the South Pacific during World War II. But I didn't have this understanding then. He was reliving the atrocities of being at war. There was no boundary between us. I could vividly see his hallucinations of the dead Japanese sniper, hung up in a tree. I was too small to understand what we were seeing, but it was raw and terrifying. My role had been to comfort my father, however I could, even though I was not more than four or five years old.

I had not thought about this, or even remembered it until now. This was what was awakened in my psyche that first night with Kent.

The next few days, when I was in the studio, trying to paint, the image of my father was all that I could see. When I tried to draw a picture, the image of the dead Japanese sniper would spill out onto the paper, in glaring, harsh black lines, signifying a rotten absence of life.

I tried to concentrate on art history class, where we were studying the Renaissance, but no matter what I did, my mind could not shake the horrible scenes. When I tried to close my eyes, to disconnect, the scene of the bedroom with my father lying across the bed, victimized by his own mind, pounded into my conscious, obliterating everything else. I didn't feel angry toward him—no, I felt fear, fear of the reality of the dead bodies hanging from the trees like fruit. There was no safe place.

My father's terror combined with my mind's own malevolent voices, and the toxic recipe was inescapable. My fragile brain could not manage this experience. I was afraid to go to sleep, fearing the images would engulf me. And being awake was no relief, especially as I quickly became sleep deprived.

I didn't know what to do.

I called Bicksey. She would know.

In jumbled fragments I told her what had happened. She suggested that I bring Kent with me to my appointment on Thursday at 4:00 p.m.

The week crawled by.

When I stood in front of a blank canvas, in my hand a paintbrush laden with Mars black paint, the only images that I could see in the white space were of human bodies, swinging by their necks from trees, with black webs rising up for the corners and edges. I could hardly stand to look at my work as I painted it. But I had to look; the work could not be painted unless I looked, over and over. There was no sense of desensitization; every time I stood back and beheld the images emerging, I felt a new rush of shock and guttural terror.

Finally, it was Thursday afternoon and Kent stuck his head through the door of my studio, where I was struggling to paint. He looked apprehensive; he just stood in the doorway, seemingly wanting to say something, but simply standing there, looking in. He could not, would not, trespass into my forbidden world.

Hand in hand, we hurriedly walked together to the counseling building. Bicksey introduced herself to Kent, who looked tense and perturbed. We went to her small office and icily sat down; there was a long painful silence. Bicksey was clearly waiting for us to start talking, but we were frozen. Finally, she started off by asking what had brought us in to see her. All at once, the scenes of my father came burning out; I relived them as I described my experiences in pressured, broken fragments of speech. Kent said nothing, looking like a deer in a hunter's scope. Bicksey just calmly sat there, not showing any signs of shock, or dismay. As I spoke, I was back in my parents' bedroom, the stricken scene of my father collapsing upon me. I was completely in it. It was so raw, so real. Eventually, the scenes from my childhood grew a little less sharp. I finally took a deep breath, and my mind came back to Bicksey's office, to the afternoon. There was no more to say—I had told it all, or at least as much as I could—it was out, and suddenly I realized the terror was no longer quite so immense.

I looked at Bicksey, registering her calm, and then with hesitation, looked over at Kent. He looked more composed. He actually seemed relieved. We looked at each other, and suddenly a slight smile flashed between us. We had survived.

Together, we had survived.

And Kent and I were in love.

"Hugging Form No.2 "
Sumi-e on rice paper
28 x 32 in.

NINE

The clouds shrouded the hills, but no, it was a
hot summer day without a cloud in the sky;
the shrouded hills were behind my eyes,
as I looked into the faces of the friends whom
I love, who are aging and growing ever closer
to crossing the high mountain pass—I saw the
clouds obscure all I love and hold dear, and
there was nothing I could do to stop it....
I closed my eyes and said thank you.

Portland, 2019

It's Sunday morning. I'm sitting in the parlor with Ananda curled up next to me. I am appreciative of the empty day stretching out in front of me.

Yesterday I made the drive south to Corvallis to see my dear friend Luma. I didn't really want to go at first, because I felt like I needed the weekend to focus on painting, but it was important to me to see her.

I've known Luma from my early days in Oregon, when I joined the Buddhist meditation group. Luma is my closest friend in Oregon, and she is a Dharma Holder, which in Zen Buddhism means that she is acknowledged as a venerable keeper and teacher of the essence of the most sacred teachings and practice. She knows me better than most other people—and she can tell me the hard truth about things when I need to hear it. There aren't too many people who can be in such a role in a person's life; it is a gift, sometimes hard to accept, but entirely priceless.

Luma is newly on the further edge of her life where she is starting to have problems with her memory. And she is painfully aware that it's happening to her. Her memory is becoming uncooperative and difficult. Her husband, Ralph, is also near to crossing the high mountain path—why can't I just say they are getting close to the end of their lives?

When I see my dear friend struggling to capture a thought or complete a sentence, I have to intentionally stop myself from filling in the blanks. I don't want to deny what is happening to her. By not denying it, I hope I am signaling that it is OK—it's just how it is.

At the other pole of my life is young Billie, the youngest student in the peer counseling class I teach. Last week, before class, I took her aside and told her that it's not appropriate to wear her T-shirt emblazoned with "Fuck You" to class. It felt strange to be in the role of telling her this—doesn't it mean I am ancient and out of touch? She explained that it is the only T-shirt without holes that she owns. I took her to my office and pulled out a brand-new, bright blue company logo tee that I had stored in a box. She immediately put it on; it fit, and she seemed glad to have it. It seems that she really didn't want to be wearing "Fuck You" either. We were both pleased.

Now I'm pondering the contents of my closet to see if there are other shirts I might give her.

There's my prized T-shirt with the image of Mexican artist Frida Kahlo—can I part with it? Maybe if I give it to Billie, she will be inspired by this famous artist—a woman who was strong and brilliantly creative. Actually, as I think about it, this is a good idea. It will be guerrilla role-modeling—covert teaching under the radar. I wonder if I can make a beneficial difference in this young woman's life. Being in the role of the teacher is a bit odd to me—it seems to suppose I know certain things. Do I really? Hmmm, not so confident about this idea. And yet, I find myself in the role of teacher often—with police officers learning to be more sensitive to people with mental illness when intervening in crises, with young psychiatrists, with the peer counseling students, and with my colleagues on the senior leadership team.

In some ways it seems natural. When I saw Luma, I remarked to her that the situation with losing her memory is a koan for her life. A koan is a Zen Buddhist question posed by life that requires an answer that is beyond rational thought, which is the essence of one's being. And, I added, she won't ever forget the most profound Truth. I could tell that she wasn't convinced. Maybe I was too facile, but perhaps I was precisely correct.

As I find myself in the role of teacher, I always have at the back of my mind the thought of what it will be like for my students if I decide I can't stand to live any longer and choose to exit the planet, to end my life. Sometimes it feels like a huge, nearly impossible conundrum. Yet, I also reflect on the idea that the Universe has placed me in this role as teacher exactly because it is not easy; maybe the closeness with which I trace the path between life and death helps give my messages a deeper meaning. So here I am, on a Sunday morning in autumn, mired in thoughts of "What if I can't stay here?"—and "I *must* stay here."

I get another cup of coffee, and for a moment I'm aware of the pale-yellow morning light streaming through the window, lighting up the room. Isn't this precious—isn't this moment of quiet beauty not to be taken for granted? But then my mind goes back to my mundane plans for later in the day, for the upcoming week, and I once more am oblivious to the rapturous sight. But not entirely oblivious.

Last Saturday I joined a group of artists whose mission is to paint grand old trees around Portland that are in danger of being cut down. The idea is to go to the actual place where the trees are growing, and paint right there on the spot, not in the studio, not from a picture—but to be with the trees in real time, and experience them at an immediate, deep level. This kind of painting outside is called *plein air*, a fancy French word for doing it on the spot, for sharing the breath of the objects to be painted. The hope is that painting these trees will help save them from certain execution. I had never painted with this group before, but they were going to paint two giant fir trees in my neighborhood, so I figured I would try it. I prepared by getting the perfect supplies ahead of time—a portable, aluminum easel, sticks of compressed oil paint that are kind of like big crayons, and a palette that is easy to carry. In the middle of the night before, when I couldn't sleep, I prepared a large canvas by painting a dark green acrylic underpainting. When Saturday morning arrived, the underpainting was dry, so I gathered everything up and trekked up the street to where the trees stand. Seven or eight painters were already there, hard at work. I walked behind them and quietly observed their canvases. They didn't acknowledge me at all. They obviously didn't want to be interrupted. I sensed that one older man who had a bushy gray beard was irritated by my presence, but maybe I misread him. I found a spot on the grass between the street and the sidewalk, nearly in front of the two giant trees, and set up my easel.

My canvas was much too big for the portable metal easel, but I managed to prop it up a little bit. Then, I leaned over, bending my knees so that I was down low, and reached out over the canvas, and in my hand, a thick cadmium red oil stick. At once I began a loose dance painting the gestures of the life force of the trees. I didn't stop to think about it all; I just moved over the surface of the canvas, making broad, brightly colored swaying and looping lines. It was not my goal to create a painting that looked exactly like the tall, deep green trees. No, I was after the very energy of the trees' essence. I lost touch with everything around me, except the trees themselves. Finally, a young woman who was trying to organize the painting event approached me and I paused. She stood looking at my canvas, and I sensed that she was perplexed.

"Well, it's big," she hesitantly began. Yes, it obviously was a big canvas—much larger than any of the other artists'. And it was obviously in a very different style than the work of the other artists, who were carefully trying to make their paintings look like realistic representations.

I looked at her and felt sympathy, because I wasn't trying to present her with a problem—I was simply doing the painting that the trees demanded of me. It wasn't my goal to fit in with the other artists in the group. Oh well, I thought, I have faith in my painting, even though she does not. And I felt light and free, because I knew my painting had a sort of integrity, even as it was electric and intense.

I'm so glad that in art school I learned to deal with other people's criticism and dour opinions—and to proceed with my work despite them.

Santa Cruz, 1988

Was it possible for me to somehow have a "regular life"—did I dare?

It was clear Kent and I loved each other.

After a year of dating, we decided the next logical step was to marry. It seemed like the obvious and inevitable thing to do.

In preparation for our wedding, we studied various cultural traditions of wedding ceremonies, because we wanted our day to be completely ours, and not reflect traditional practices that imply that women are owned by men.

It was finally the August day of our ceremony. We stood in a park under immense oak and spruce trees. The Irish band with fiddle and harp started playing, and I walked down the aisle, alone, to be married. No man was giving me away. I own myself, so how could anyone give me away? As I walked down the aisle, the Celtic harp played an Irish war march, a tune that ironically my forebears had heard as they marched into battle hundreds of years ago.

I was trying not to walk too fast. I could see Kent standing there, underneath the biggest oak tree, waiting for me, in his grey tux, so handsome, incredibly tall, smiling, what a sight—my heart soared.

We said our vows, which we had spent weeks writing ourselves. Lisa stood next to me, and we both were tearing up. Ava read a poem about a whale spout being a halo over our heads.

It was done. Kent and I kissed.

Music, applause. Our friends and family surrounded us.

Bicksey was there. Old friends came from Texas, Kent's family, my brother, who had actually traded in his overalls for a suit. My wild artist girlfriends from art school were all there, including one who even brought her dog.

There were flowers everywhere. My mother was really happy; everyone started making toasts. Little kids danced jigs to the music. Everyone hugged, and sipped champagne.

I looked over at Kent and saw how beautiful he was. It was hard to believe such a wonderful thing was happening to me.

Finally, Kent and I drove away in his pickup truck, with "Just Married!!!" written in white shoe polish across the back.

Kent and I were in Hawaii on our honeymoon. I was in the hotel room, sitting on the bed. I looked around me, and I felt more like a prisoner than a guest.

I had not brought any psych medication with us. I didn't plan to need medication on my honeymoon. Honeymoons are supposed to be delicious and ideal—I certainly wouldn't need medication in Paradise!

But there was a problem. I did need it—even though in mind I shouldn't.

Kent and I talked about trying to call a local doctor for a prescription. I decided to just tough it out. It was so beautiful on Kauai—snorkeling in the blue green waters, walking on the white sands, colors of the fish in the coral reef, the music and dancing at night.

But inside I was fighting.

It was exquisite and lush, but the sights and sounds pounded through my senses like knives. I couldn't modulate how the sensations entered into me. I had no defenses or way to screen out the sensations that flooded my senses. Everything, even the most seemingly marvelous things, came painfully blasting in. I knew that Kent had no idea of this. I tried to tell him about what I was experiencing. But I knew he couldn't understand.

I felt like I needed to be in a small quiet place—I needed a cocoon. There were too many jagged edges. I didn't care if it was called Paradise; it hurt to be there.

On the last day of our honeymoon, Kent and I went body surfing out in the waves. When we emerged from the water there was a shock: Kent's new gold wedding ring was gone. It had been washed off his finger by the waves. We sat down upon the sand and just stared at his bare hand. It became suddenly very clear: there was no way to protect us from losing the things we valued—nothing was hallowed, or safe. We held onto each other's hand and sat, without speaking. This was our lesson.

Back in Santa Cruz, Kent and I lived in an apartment on Felker Street. It was a small place, near downtown. I painted on a small table easel in the living room.

Kent worked the swing shift over the mountain at a computer company. I had a part-time job as a clerk in an art supply. The pattern of life settled in.

I was a wife.

I had a husband.

This is my life.

It was a little life.

In this little apartment.

I could look out the window and see homeless people under the bridge.

I made a painting of what I saw.

It was hard to make sense of this life. I loved my husband, but I didn't see him much.

He came home so late and I went to work so early at the art store.

At work I ran my fingers over the bristles of the paintbrushes. I loved to touch them. I knew everything about them. I knew everything about all of the different kinds of paint. I knew everything about all the different kinds of drawing paper. I was so happy when someone came into the store who needed my help. I was so happy when there was a question that I could answer for someone.

But for so many hours, there was little meaning or purpose. The hours crept by.

I started sinking down. Where was the purpose, the meaning?

Sinking down. This little life I was leading. Was leading down.

I was going down, down, down.

I was at the bottom. There was no way up. There was no way out.

But one.

I had been married for nearly a year. I loved my husband, but I had no choice. I couldn't stand to be on the planet. There simply was no way to continue to live.

I drove my car north up the coast.

I knew what I had to do.

I pulled off the road at Davenport, onto a lookout place where I had always watched the gray whales on their annual migration. I loved to watch them every spring when they would brilliantly breach into the air, sending strong spouts of their breath out into the sun.

But this was different. There was no joy here now.

I got the bag of full pill bottles out of my trunk.

I took a piece of paper. All I could find to write with was a piece of black drawing charcoal.

"Dear Kent, I'm sorry. I do love you. M."

I started taking the pills, washing them down with a bottle of diet coke.

I was sorry. More pills. Please let this be over. More pills. I am so bad to be doing this. More pills. The voices were yelling DIE -DIE -DIE!

Just the voices…

Dark.

Bare awareness of something happening in a fog far away someplace—people vaguely shouting.

I was barely awake. I didn't know where I was. I went back to sleep.

Suddenly awake. A woman was next to me, speaking. "Do you know where you are?"

No.

"Good Samaritan Hospital in Santa Cruz. Do you remember what happened?"

No, not really.

"You took some pills."

Yeah. I guess I did. And?

"After the drugs wore off some, in the morning, you drove your car into oncoming traffic. You hit an oncoming car. You caused an accident."

A feeling of sick panic suddenly flooded through me. I felt a rush of terror.

Had I killed anyone?

A long pause. Adrenalin was pouring through me.

"No, no one was hurt. You've been in and out of consciousness for the past two days."

Relief swept through me—I didn't kill anyone!! Thank God!

The enormity of what I had done and how close I came to hurting or killing another human being shook me to my core. It was one thing to kill myself, but to have nearly killed someone else, this repelled me.

I had done this terrible thing. I could have killed somebody, but I was spared an experience worse than any I could imagine.

Shaken to my core. Totally shaken.

I was back home now.

A meeting was held at the little apartment on Felker Street. It was so that everyone who I cared about and who cared about me could tell me how they felt about what I did. I had let them all down.

Bicksey was there. My psychiatrist was here. Lisa and her husband were there.

And, of course Kent was there.

They went around the circle telling me about how my actions had hurt them. I just sat there, listening to all of them. I had no defense, no excuse. I knew I would have to do better. But in my heart, I had no idea how I was going to do it. I had zero defense.

I weakly tried to convince them that I had turned over a new leaf—it was obviously what I was expected to say. But inside I was feeling remote. A huge wall was closing around me. It was like I was looking down from the ceiling at the sorry scene in the living room. I was suspended in the air; the scene was stuck, it played over and over.

I was apologizing. Over and over.

I was truly sorry. I would do better. But it was impossible. They did not understand. Things were so impossible.

I would try; I really would.

But I didn't have hope. I didn't tell them that, about not having hope.

It was so grim.

I walked to work at the art store every day. I had to walk because I had lost my driver's license for six months.

It took over two hours to get there.

Some days I rode the bus. I was doing penance for my sin.

I was trying to be better for Kent.

I was trying to be better for everyone that I hurt. Trying, trying, trying.

Kent agreed that we could get a dog.

At the animal shelter, I knew the dog immediately. She was sandy-colored, shaggy, medium-sized. Big brown eyes… when I heard her deep, resonant bark, I knew at once that this was the dog for me.

I named her Iris. Iris and I had a deep bond from the beginning. She started making me very happy. Kent and I had moved to a little house near a wild park. It was now the three of us.

Iris and I took long walks in the woods. I planted purple statice flowers and bamboo.

The garage became my studio. I began to work on gigantic charcoal drawings, as big as the walls. A handful of charcoal. I jumped up and hurled my loaded fist at the paper. Made contact, then dragged the velvet, black mark across the white. Black dust on my face and hands. I did the work. Images got pulled out, punched in. Some were delicate; others lurched out boldly. Sweaty and dirty, real work. The drawings were huge. It suited me. The images were dark. And dark was what was truthful for me.

"Feeling Jagged with Cadmium"
Oil on canvas
30 x 40 in.

TEN

We move through the air because we can,
we can see through the leaves of the tree that
the neighbors are building things with their
hands, we whistle, and our dog comes running;
do not try to tell me that the fountain of
miracles has dried up.

Portland, 2019

The holidays are finally over, and now January is pounding the faintly light days into long dark nights. I went to San Antonio to celebrate Christmas with my mother, who is now living in an assisted living facility. I detest traveling during the holidays, but she said, "This will be our last Christmas together." How could I object?

I worried that she would disapprove of me since I have gained weight again, and because of the thousand other reasons I don't measure up. But when I hugged her, her only words were that she loves me, and is proud of me. And isn't this everything—and why is it always such a surprise to hear these words? She is ninety-five now. She was in hospice care for eight months, but she stubbornly refused to die, so they kicked her out. She is a tough old Texas woman, and she has survived her life with grit and gumption. Every time I see her now, I wonder if it is the "last time?" But she is on her own time schedule, and it is mysterious and unpredictable. She says she is ready for her life to be done, but somehow her body has other ideas.

When I hugged her, she felt so small and frail, yet her fire and personality are huge. Now I just bow to her autonomy and will.

When I look at her face, I can see how we look alike—everyone says we do—and I am struck by the mystery of our connection. When we said "goodbye," we both wept.

Yesterday I had a new rocking chair delivered. The delivery man asked me to show him the room where he should take it, and I led the way up the stairs to the dark green room I affectionately call "The Writer's Lair." After about fifteen minutes of unwrapping the chair from its bountiful layers of plastic, we came back down the stairs—and then the shock: the front door was gaping wide open—it had not been closed when we went upstairs. Immediately a surge of panic went through me—where was Ananda?! I ran out to the street; there was no sight of her, just cars speeding by.

"Ananda!" I called, over and over, down the sidewalk, running back to the house and through all the rooms, and still no sight of her.

"Ananda!" I cried and ran out the kitchen door to the back yard and garden. And then, my heart soared as I saw her rounding the corner of the house, ears out, gleeful, bounding up and down through the winter mud.

We were saved!

San Jose, 1990

My life teetered between extremes.

I taught a drawing class at the university where I also attended art school. This role of instructor felt good to me—sharing my love of drawing. I loved my students, I loved to draw, so it felt natural to teach them about something that I love.

But then:

Again, voices were ripping at me, condemning me.

I took an extra pill. Maybe it would make the voices quiet down.

Maybe.

I never knew what would work. I never knew what I could count on. I never knew when there were going to be voices. I couldn't rely on my brain.

This made it very hard sometimes, especially on days when I had to teach. Some days it was impossible. Somehow. Everything would fall apart, but I just kept pulling it together, again and again. That was how it was getting done. In bits and pieces. Forward then backwards. I always slid back, but I always then pushed forward.

Finally, the day of my oral examination for my master of fine arts degree arrived.

I wasn't too nervous, just a little. The committee asked me questions about my work.

My huge charcoal drawings filled the gallery.

I answered each question. I defended my work. It felt good. I took pride in seeing it hanging there.

I believe in my work.

I can stand up for it.

I passed the exam.

The degree was mine—Master of Fine Arts.

This was a sweet victory.

Kent and I, and Iris, moved to a tiny duplex near downtown. The little house I loved next to the park was too expensive, so we had to move. We were now stuffed into two small rooms, with Iris. Here, I felt caged like a panther in a zoo. In a cage that was too small.

There was no place to go. There was no place.

Except, there sort of was *one* place.

We lived downtown near the Zen Center. It was a place of meditation. I walked there nearly every day at dusk. I sat on a round black cushion facing the wall. There were other people there, sitting in a row, all of us silently doing the same thing. We were doing zazen. A deep gong sounded, three times. We sat in the cross-legged position.

Very still.

Very quiet. Except very loud inside my mind.

I tried to still my mind. Most of the time it was impossible. Sometimes there were voices.

But I just sat there. I didn't move. Silence, inside the noise of my mind.

Time passed. Finally, the gong sounded again. Meditation was over.

This time was like a raft in the middle of a stormy sea.

I got up and slowly walked home, to the too-small place: the place that couldn't hold me, my husband, and my dog. This place where we lived had no room for me to make art. Iris had no place to be outside. I felt trapped.

I was at my mother's house in Texas.

I had Iris with me.

I couldn't stay in that little apartment with Kent any longer. He was still there while we figured out what to do. There was a chance to get transferred to a job in Corvallis,

Oregon. Maybe we would move north. I had heard it was green there. There were mountains. There was the ocean, wild beaches, animals…

I was thinking about all of this. Was there the possibility of hope?

While in San Antonio I started seeing a psychiatrist for medication. He put me on a new schizophrenia drug. I had to get a blood test every week. He was excited about this new drug and thought it was perfect for me. It made me sleepy, but I took it anyway.

Then I noticed that I was drooling a little bit. Liquid would seep out, unbidden, out of the corners of my mouth if I didn't pay attention. Just another side effect. I would just have to accept it, even though it was unacceptable.

I was really annoyed, and it was embarrassing, too. It was impossible to pretend to be a regular person when I had to constantly be on guard for drooling.

But this was just how it was. I knew that I had to put up with it. I would have to concentrate on not drooling when I was with other people.

Then, the decision was made: We were moving to Oregon.

Life would be better there. We would start over.

Starting over, moving forward.

I would see if Oregon held answers for my life.

"Detail, Human Being, Male No. 1"
Pen and ink on paper
42 x 72 in.

ELEVEN

*Late at night the wind started blowing and
in the vast navy-blue universe we held our
frozen fingers, crossed in a divine sign, a mudra,
a symbol of profound protection, for out in the
significantly weightless air the night birds flew
on their sacred routes across the moon,
and we were saved.*

Portland, 2019

It's Sunday evening and Ananda and I just took our evening walk in the neighborhood. The blessed weekend is nearly over.

I remember very well how it was when I was not able to work and was on federal assistance called SSI and disability. I dreaded the times when people who didn't know me would innocently ask me, "So what do you do?" I usually could not bring myself to say that I didn't work because I had a mental health disability. I just didn't want to say it, even though it was the truth. I would usually talk about being an artist, which was also true, but it wasn't how I made my living, and I knew I was only telling a small part of the story. Every month I used to get the small check from the government. It wasn't enough for me to come close to living at the poverty line. I knew I didn't deserve more. This was how it was. I had bought into the stigma, even though I would never have admitted it and didn't really understand how I was adding to a negative stereotype.

Now, I work as a senior director for peer services in a big behavioral health organization, plus I'm on the faculty of the psychiatry department of a medical school, so some people assume I couldn't possibly really have a serious and persistent mental illness—it just doesn't fit the usual stereotype. I understand—I have to deal with this frequently. In fact, a big part of my work involves encouraging people to have new, more enlightened ideas about what is possible for people who have been diagnosed. I personally have a new psychiatrist, and she told me that maybe my diagnosis of schizophrenia is not correct. Perhaps it is too unexpected that I have my occupation and can do the things I do. I'm going to get a new assessment by a clinical psychologist who will determine what the truth is.

Leading up to the assessment, I am excited and wondering if I might get excellent news that I don't have a terrible disease. What would that mean, anyway? Would it be good, or bad? I'm also wondering what that would mean with the dozens of times I've been hospitalized? Has it all somehow been a mistake? If I don't have schizophrenia, then what is the explanation for everything that I have gone through?

On the day of the assessment, I left work early and drove to the clinic. The psychologist met me in the waiting room, and we went back to his office. I noticed that he seemed very nice, maybe more helpful than I expected him to be. Did I expect him to be rude? No, but this was not a pleasant social visit, so why should we even act like it is?

He proceeded to ask me pages of questions about my life, all the experiences of when I was little, about when I first started hearing voices, all the stories of the hospitalizations, the suicide attempts, the extreme experiences of running through the forest at night, about how I can't shut out noises from my too-sensitive brain. He asked question after question, and I made a point to look him in the eyes when I answered. I was as accurate and precise as possible in my answers—I wanted the results to be 100 percent correct. Finally, he gave me some printed pages of questions I was to score. I did this very quickly, not wanting to think about the answers—I just wanted to get it done as speedily as possible. I noticed that some of the questions were asked repeatedly, but with slightly different wording. Finally, I finished. I knew I had told the truth, and whatever would come, it would just be what it was.

Two weeks later, I returned to the clinic to get the results. I was anxious but also eager. I sat across the desk from the psychologist and waited for him to begin speaking. I wanted to hear his report, but I was prepared for the worst, whatever it might be. I leaned forward.

The psychologist said three different things: the first was he found "no evidence of pathology" based on the test where I had to score the pages of questions. It didn't mean that I didn't have a very serious psychiatric illness—it just meant that I was doing so much better now that on the standardized test, my responses showed that I have healed in some respects. Exclamation! No pathology! A miracle! Yay! My life now is beyond what anyone had ever predicted for me. I had defied the dire expectations.

Next, he quickly added that I have schizo-affective disorder, in remission, and post-traumatic stress disorder.

Schizo-affective disease is kind of like a combination of schizophrenia and bipolar disorder. It would explain the voices, but also the nights of running through the forest, unable to stop or sleep. The PTSD, he said, was from the treatments like Cathexis and sometimes when I was physically restrained against my will in the hospital.

So, the biggest news is no current pathology, but then the part about being in remission puts all the years of the voices, hospitalizations, shock treatments, and extreme measures into context.

One important message in all of this is that it is possible to be very stricken with a psychiatric disease—one of the very worst—but to recover and heal from it. It isn't the death sentence that is commonly assumed. No, it is possible to have it, and then heal, and then go on to thrive! It's not a simple straight line, and it's not like everything becomes rosy. No. Still, things are possible that no one had ever even dared to suggest. An enormous life is possible! I'm not saying that everything is easy now. But I am saying that it is possible to go beyond the limits that scores of doctors had set for me. I honestly don't know how things will end up with my life. But right now, I am finding possibilities that no one ever imagined for me.

I went back to my office and immediately went to see my friend and colleague, Will, who is a psychiatrist. "No pathology—I now have no pathology!" I incredulously informed him.

"Welcome to neurosis, like the rest of us!" he chirped.

"Oh, no! Not me! I have zero—zip—pathology. I did not trade in psychosis to be neurotic!"

I am adamant about this.

Corvallis, Oregon, 1992

Was it possible to start over—or was it an illusion that would swallow me up into another black pit?

Kent and I arrived in Corvallis, a small college town where we first needed to stay in a motel until we could get settled and buy a house. I wasn't able to have Iris in the motel with us, so I boarded her with a woman who raised chickens right outside town. Many chickens, dozens of them...everywhere. In exchange for her keeping Iris for me, I would go and collect and wash chicken eggs. The eggs were brown and very dirty; it was a new experience to gather them in a bucket and scrub them with a brush. I did this three times each week. Kent and I started searching for a new home. The houses that we could afford in Corvallis just didn't have the right feeling. They were too bland. Just boxes. Finally, our real estate agent took us on a long drive south of town to a little village in the middle of acres of Christmas tree farms. It was called Alpine. There she showed us a small frame house with two giant ponderosa pines in the front yard. These massive trees were like sentinels, guarding the house. I immediately knew this was the right place for us. We were finally home, all three of us.

We started our new lives in Oregon.

I made a studio in the garage and planted rosemary plants along the rough edges of the gravel driveway.

Kent worked swing shift at the computer warehouse, and I taught a drawing class at the community college. But things were not easy.

The voices were never far away from my mind. I needed to see a psychiatrist to prescribe medication—the one that made me drool, and that required weekly blood tests. I enrolled in a local day treatment program.

On Sunday mornings, I would go to a Zen meditation group. I would show up and not say a word to anyone else there. No one had any idea that during the week, I was in the role of a mental patient in a day treatment program. When I would sit trying to meditate, the voices would climb out of my unconscious and billow across my awareness. I just sat there, trying to be still, trying to focus on my breath, but the minutes between the soundings of the gong were strewn out near the limits of what I could endure. But somehow, I had a strange sense that meditating was precisely what I needed to do, even though I was never sure if I would make it to the next gong.

Kent and I started to drift apart. There was tension between us.

Part of it was how often I was in the hospital.

Our insurance covered only one hundred days of hospitalization for mental illness, and I had exceeded the lifetime number. If I had had heart disease or cancer, there wouldn't be a limit—but because it was mental illness, it was different.

I could tell that this was putting stress on him.

I knew that when he married me, he had no idea it would be like this. I felt like I was bringing him down.

But he didn't complain.

We never fought.

But distance between us was growing.

Kent continued to pursue his love of music. He was often going away on the weekends to numerous folk and bluegrass music festivals. It started to become evident that we were on different paths. We never had arguments. No, we just stopped communicating at all. After a long weekend away at a music festival in the Sierras, Kent returned and casually mentioned to me that he had gone bird-watching with a woman named Leticia. I expressed surprise because he had never expressed any interest in birds or bird-watching. Suddenly he was a bird-watcher? I questioned. He was crushed by my response. His new friend, Leticia, was the one who understood his soul. She started to call our house and ask for him on our phone. I suddenly realized my husband was having an extramarital affair. I was confused but furious at once. When I answered the phone, and it was her, I angrily told her to stop calling my husband.

Our marriage was falling apart.

We were trying to talk it through one morning in the kitchen. Kent stood across the sunlit room, by the stove. On the table, in front of me, was a piece of china. It was a dinner plate, a fine Limoges porcelain plate; the pattern was called Artois Bleu. It was white with small blue flowers and a circle of real gold around the edge. I had selected the pattern for us before we had been married. This china was originally designed for the French monarch Louis XVI himself, in 1781. It was made with special clay called kaolin. It was a beautiful and refined object. But here I was, feeling hot rage toward Kent, for our unworkable lives together and our unworkable lives apart. I reached my hand down toward the plate, to grasp it, and for a moment, I felt I would pick it up and hurl it across the room toward Kent, so it would shatter—not to hit him with it, but to underscore the enormity of my pain. I would destroy this plate, and it would be a symbol of how our lives had fallen apart.

But I paused. I simply could not destroy this beautiful, innocent object, even if it would be the dramatic gesture that the situation seemed to require. It was simply too beautiful. The elegant plate remained untouched. Everything else broke apart.

Kent left.

It was over.

"Deliverance (No.13)"
Charcoal on paper
30 x 40 in.

TWELVE

*The brilliant green moss on the rock beckons
her to stroke it, and as she dips her fingers into
its luscious hair, her day becomes much lighter,
and deeper into the realm of her core;
the stone sighs and we are all better for it.*

Portland, 2019

My young peer counseling student Billie asked to talk with me after class yesterday. We went to my office, and I closed the door to give us privacy. She sat across the room, staring down at her shoes, somehow searching for a way to begin. I sat, trying to communicate patience and acceptance to her. I wanted her to feel safe to confide in me, whatever she needed to say. As I watched her, I realized she was beginning to shake, and her tears were not far behind.

She took a deep breath and began telling me the story of Tim, the man with whom she had fallen in love. She said he had become deeply depressed, and she was very worried about him but didn't know how to help him, or if it was even possible for him to get better. Tim also had gone back to using meth and other drugs, and when he was high, he lost all contact with reality. He even had hit her last Friday night, when she tried to stop him from walking out the door.

I listened to her story, aware of how it was one I had heard variations on since I had been working in the behavioral health program. I was aware that there was no easy answer to tell her: take care of herself, keep reaching out, here's the number for the crisis response team, hope and pray for his safety. I wrote up a list of numbers to call if needed, but mostly I just listened and bore witness to her pain. The one thing I could do was let her know I heard her sorrow. I wanted to communicate to her that she was not alone in her predicament. I was painfully aware of the fact that I couldn't offer her any big solutions. But I was there with her in the deepest sense. It wasn't enough, but it was real.

Alpine, Oregon, 1996

I was a woman with a dog—would I be able to make a new life, or was I just going to be dragged underwater and finally drown?

Kent had moved out, and the details of our divorce were left to the lawyers.

I stayed in the little house, but it swallowed me up in my solitariness. A deep depression grew over me and consumed me. The yard of the little house grew covered in weeds, foot-tall grass, and invasive, thorny wild berry vines. When Iris was out in the yard, the weeds and grass were so high above her head that she simply disappeared.

The voices pounded at me, and I found myself hospitalized frequently. I would stop eating and not take my medication unless I was forced. I was repeatedly put in a seclusion room with my ankles and wrists tied down with thick leather restraints, and a camera recording me lying there.

During one of those times, when I was tied down in four-point restraint, an orderly named Carl, who was supposed to be watching me, verbally threatened to put a tube down my nose so I would be forced to take food. He said he would tie me into a chair in the dayroom and do it where everyone else could watch. Terror shot through me, and I screamed for my very life. Later, when I talked to my doctor, he said this would never happen. Carl had made it all up, just because I was vulnerable, and he had the power to act out his sadism.

Carl disappeared. I wondered if he had been fired from his job. No one ever mentioned him again.

The longest I spent in four-point restraint was twenty-three hours. Although it was physically painful to be tied down like that for so long, it was also a relief to not have to try to control myself. I could struggle and fight, and it didn't matter. Nothing mattered.

My existence had become extreme, one that is entirely foreign to most people. At least unfamiliar to most middle-class white people, like me. Now I am realizing that plenty of people in our society whose skin is brown or black, especially if they are poor, have variations of being forcibly restrained within the context of our criminal justice system. Being treated this way was a shock to me personally. Now I feel compelled to note that for some people in our society and in some other parts of the world, it is neither unusual nor avoidable. Being tied down against my will for hours is an experience like none other that I know. All I can say is that now I can appreciate the fact that having been in this situation gives me a tiny bit of understanding and empathy for what it feels like—although, of course, because of my whiteness and social class, I can really only grasp a small part of it.

When I was home, I began a destructive pattern of behavior: I would start by taking a few of my various pills, and then drink wine, then more pills, then more wine. It was impulsive, and the more wine and pills I took, the easier it became to take more. I would eventually be on the edge of losing consciousness. Right before totally passing out, I would call my psychiatrist's or therapist's office. Someone would send out the sheriff's deputies and ambulance crew, and they would break down the front door, load me up in the ambulance, and deliver me to the emergency department of the hospital in Corvallis. At the emergency department, they would perform gastric lavage—the nice French term for pumping out my stomach.

I was just conscious enough to hear the nurse saying to the doctor, "How disgusting!" She said it. I heard it. The doctor agreed. And it was true. I was disgusting, to her, to him, and most of all, to myself.

Variations on this scene repeated over and over. It was the one predictable experience in my life.

Everyone grew very weary of it—my doctor, my therapist, the ER personnel, the deputies, and most of all, I did. And I knew in my heart there would come a time when the deputies and ambulance crew wouldn't get there in time. I would surely be dead. Was this really what I wanted?

Out of the hospital, I was back to my life, and my dog. Every day I felt the pull to do it again.

To buy another bottle of wine, take more pills.

I wanted to have that feeling of the pain just easing away, to just have that feeling of nothing matters.

There was just so much pain. It was more than I could bear. I wanted it to go away.

The wine and the pills seemed to make it ease up.

I repeated this scene so many times.

One afternoon I went to the grocery store at the corner to buy another bottle of wine.

I would need it to potentiate the pills I was going to take that night, and then maybe die.

Sandy, who worked there, knew I had this problem with the overdoses.

She knew that the ambulance came to my house often because of the wine and the pills.

And here I was at the store to buy another bottle of wine.

But Sandy said no, in a friendly way, but firm. "Here's a cappuccino on the house," she told me. She handed me a giant cup of the luscious hot drink.

I was deeply moved. She had taken a stand on behalf of my life. She told me no. She would not participate in me killing myself.

Because of Sandy, I would not drink wine and take pills that night.

This meant a lot to me—she had expressed acknowledgment of my pained behavior, and had not judged me, but at the same time she had been unwilling to simply look the other way.

This said something profound to me. Somehow, it meant that she cared.

It was another night.

This time I had gone too far.

The sheriff's deputies came, now the fire department, now the ambulance.

They all knew me.

Everything was fading fast.

How fast would they be able to get me to the hospital this time?

Would it be fast enough?

I knew I was playing a game. I knew the stakes were high.

I was detached from it all as they worked to save my life.

I was fading out, my life was fading, I was watching it fade.

I was so far away. I was watching, looking down on the scene.

They put me on the stretcher and took me out to the ambulance.

It was another ride, just another ride.

A race that I didn't care to win.

But on some level, I did care.

I cared a great deal.

"Why do you do this to yourself?" the doctor later asked.

I can't stand the pain; there is just so much pain.

Pain from what?

Everything. It's all so painful.

That's all there is.

I was out of the hospital. I was on a ton of medication. I weighed more than I've ever weighed in my life—a side effect of the medication. I was still trying to have some semblance of a life.

It helped to go to the Zen group on Sundays. Somehow this seemed to be a way forward.

In one way I was leading a double life—I would try to destroy my life, but at other times I was practicing meditation and nonviolence.

After much thought and reflection, I came to the realization that I wanted to make a deeper commitment to studying and practicing this way of compassion and nonviolence. I realized that it was really a choice between life and death. I pondered this very hard. This was an immense question of which the answer required my deepest honesty. The answer was in no way evident.

After much thought, I somehow decided to choose to live. I didn't feel confident in my decision—could I even do this? But I would put my energy into going forward with it.

I made a special trip to Portland to ask Chozen, the leader of the Zen group, to be my teacher. I asked her and she said yes.

I told her that I wanted to take the Precepts, the Buddhist vows. In Zen Buddhism, this is a sort of lay ordination. She agreed to help me.

I spent the next six months preparing myself. I had to sew a special indigo blue cloth, called a *rakusu,* to wear around my neck. My hands shook so badly from the medication that I couldn't sew with the needle and thread. A kind woman named Mushin from the local meditation group sewed it for me while I lay on her sofa, basically useless.

Finally, it was time for the ceremony, time for me to take the Precepts. It had been months since I had started to pursue this path.

This was a Big Deal.

I felt solemn, nervous, excited, and determined, all at once.

All of my friends from the Zen group were there.

Chozen, the teacher, was there. My friends Luma, Katie, and Mushin were there. During the special ceremony I was supposed to make full ritual bows all the way to the floor, but I was too overweight to go to the floor, so I had to compromise and make standing bows.

That would have to be good enough. It was time to say my vows.

"I vow not to harm life."

I bowed.

"I vow not to lie."

I bowed.

"I vow not to abuse alcohol or drugs."

I bowed.

There were ten precepts in all. I said them all and bowed each time.

As I heard myself making these solemn vows, these commitments, I realized I must deeply change my life. I stood there, in front of everyone.

There was no going back. I would not be able to do the same old things.

Then I said I took refuge in the *Buddha,* in the *dharma,* which means the teachings and the reality they represent, and in the *sangha,* the community of all those beings who practice the Buddha way.

Chozen sprinkled my head with an evergreen branch dipped in water. She put my new *rakusu,* the bib-like indigo sewn cloth, over my head. It was an abbreviated version of a Buddhist robe.

Part of the taking of the vows meant that I was given a new Buddhist name.

Usually it's just one name, but Chozen said she had actually given me two names.

The first is Jisho, which means compassion for all living things. She said it means I must have compassion for myself, too.

The next name is Ahimsa, which is Sanskrit and means non-harming.

I heard these names. I understood their relevance. They were selected for me because of my potential to grow and express the value and qualities of compassion and non-harming. I took them into myself and claimed them as my own. I was glad for them.

At the same time, I realized how little confidence I had that I could live up to them.

I received them as a gift, and I felt grateful to my teacher.

She said a blessing in Japanese.

The group leader, Mushin, led me around the room before the circle of all the group's members, and as I passed, each bowed to me. What a feeling it was, to have everyone bowing; I was so moved and amazed. I felt a deep life change had come over me, and that everyone in the group was acknowledging and celebrating my change.

When the ceremony was over everyone hugged me. One young woman took a picture of the group with me in the middle, surrounded by my friends and my teacher. I was smiling really big.

I now had these new names to live up to.

"Compassion for all living things."

"Non-harming."

There must be something in me, something that is capable of these attributes. How was I going to find the non-harming in me when I wanted to destroy myself? Where would I find compassion when the voices were telling me that I must die?

I didn't have the answers to these questions, but my teacher said it was fine to not know all the answers.

Later, the urges to self-destruct kept coming. My new Buddhist names did not magically mean that I was somehow freed from my urge toward self-destruction. But now I started holding back from acting on the impulses.

I was still so unhappy with my life.

There was still so much pain. I still felt compelled to destroy myself.

But a new force was urging me on at the same time. Something was pulling me toward life. Sometimes it was weaker, but other times I could feel it strongly coursing through my veins. Sometimes it was so faint that I could hardly tell it was there at all.

I was a little reluctant to call it hope, but this was something new.

I was opening to the possibility of hope.

There finally came a day, in late winter, when after a sleepless night I wearily walked through the house to the living room, which had become my studio. There was a contemporary Buddhist magazine randomly lying open on the table; I happened to notice an article about lotus flowers. I picked it up, and absently started reading it. Lotuses are considered sacred and holy in Asia. The article described how lotuses have to have their roots in the mud, and only if their roots are immersed in mud can they grow and be beautiful. It further explained how, when scientists took forty lotus plants and hooked them up to a special electrical apparatus, those forty lotuses had enough energy to illuminate a lightbulb—just with their sheer life energy.

Those lotuses were filled with the life force.

I slowly put the magazine down.

Deep in my gut a vast question formed before me.

What did this mean for my life?

I picked up a thick paintbrush and buried it into a blob of cadmium red paint. I took the fully loaded brush and advanced it on the large white empty canvas in front of me. I drew the shape of a lotus, a red lotus. Then I took a new brush, dipped it in raw umber, and started to form the mud around the bloom. The background of the mud became alive and charged with organic energy.

A picture began to emerge.

Finally, I stood back.

In front of me was a new painting: a red lotus surrounded by its rich organic mud. The flower was beautiful, but the most remarkable part of the painting was the dynamic mud.

I stared at it. This mud was the suffering of my life. I had more mud in my life than anything else. My mud—was this the key to the beauty of my life?

I could not have the beauty of the lotus unless I embraced the mud. My mud—my pain—could this be the vehicle to a new way of being?

Excitement and joy suddenly coursed through me.

I realized I had discovered my life force.

I would embrace this image of the lotus and its mud, and by painting it, over and over, I would embrace myself and channel my life force into my will to live.

Suddenly, a brave new hope had taken hold of me, in the form of the lotus in the mud: my mud flower.

I began to paint canvas after canvas of lotus images. They took various forms; some looked like recognizable flowers, but others were more loosely constructed. Some paintings were in yellows, golds, and greens, while others were only black, white, and red. Some canvases were big, but some were small. Always I painted the mud with extra care. I wanted to explore every possible shape, color, and mood of lotuses. Each painting was a vehicle for delving into and expressing my life force. The simple act of painting the mud flowers made the energy of life rise up in the core of my body.

I stopped the pattern of overdoses and suicide attempts. My approach to my life had changed. What is it, when a person has new eyes and has made a new decision deeply in their soul's root, that then the way one sees oneself becomes different, and even beyond this, the world begins to reveal a new side of itself as well?

My eyes were new. I started to look for a new response from the world.

And it came.

One day I was sitting in the dismal waiting room at the day treatment program I regularly attended. I had an appointment later with my case manager. It was a predictably shabby and depressing room, with plastic chairs and outdated magazines. Among the ancient magazines, I noticed an unusual publication. It was actually a newsletter for a professional organization about brain research. I had never seen it before. It was odd that it was even there in this environment at all; it was probably a mistake. I was curious and started to read it. On the last page there was a list of new medications under development for schizophrenia that were in the clinical trial phase. I scanned this list. My eyes stopped halfway down the page.

Here was an experimental drug that did not cause weight gain. The side effect of weight gain had always been very upsetting to me, but there had never been a way to avoid it. When I was on the schizophrenia medications, especially the newer ones, my weight would climb, and it was one of the reasons I always stopped taking them. Hmmm...but here was a medication that didn't have this side effect. Was it possible this a might be solution for me? I read every word, over and over. I started getting a feeling deep down inside that my life was about to change. I wondered if I had I discovered a key?

When I got home, I tried to find out more about the drug on the internet, but there was nothing. I did find the phone number for the company that made the drug, and I started calling it. I kept getting connected to people who had no idea of what I was asking: How could I get into a clinical trial so I could start taking this new drug? After repeated unsuccessful calls, I was frustrated, but I was completely determined to find a way—I was now convinced that I had to do it in order to heal. I had a deep sense that this new medication would be a key part of how I would find a way to get well. I can't rationally explain why I was so convinced of the necessity that I must take it, but I *knew*. It was not a magical solution, but it would provide a crucial piece of the puzzle that had been lacking.

After many calls and questions, I was finally connected to a doctor who knew something about the research. He was able to answer some of my questions about how the drug worked, and he told me there were just a handful of clinical trials going on in the United States. He said he would connect me to someone who might be able to help.

I finally reached a woman named Lois who was a big director at the drug company. She told me that the only place on the West Coast where I could be in a study and take the medication was Los Angeles. I told her I was determined to do it, and she said she would help make it possible. My psychiatrist was very surprised, but he finally agreed to the idea, and a plan was quickly put into place. My mother tried to dissuade me. She thought it was just another wild idea of mine. At first the logistics seemed impossible. But I had an incredibly strong sense that I would do it, somehow. How would I even get to Los Angeles? One of my friends told me she would pay for one of the plane tickets. Then another friend said she would pay for one. Then Lois said the drug company would pay for my airplane tickets. It was as if the universe was rolling out the royal magic carpet for me to do this. My first appointment at the hospital in LA was set for just after the new year. I could hardly wait.

I was going to find a way to become a lotus flower and to use my mud to create something beautiful. I was going to turn into a mud flower.

"Winter Lotus"
Oil on canvas
30 x 40 in.

THIRTEEN

The woman who lives in the cave builds her fire
small, so she can cozy up to it and stay in its
small arc of light—she knows outside the cave
the Big Animals are hunting for small,
soft bodies—but sometimes she must leave her
cave to gather wood for her fire;
why is it so hard to find her way across the
acres of stars, miles of shining constellations,
the omnipresent solar glare, yet longing for the
safety of that dark and quiet cave—oh why—
this is what she asked me, as I stood on the
threshold with my arms filled with flowers.

Portland, 2020

Here in Portland, actually everywhere in the world, life has suddenly turned upside down. For nearly two months we have been in lockdown due to the coronavirus pandemic. I'm fortunate to be able to work from home, and to have a place to live and food to eat. Much of the world is just barely hanging on. The governor has ordered everyone to stay home, except to go grocery shopping, or to go outside, so long as we stay six feet apart from everyone else and wear a mask over our nose and mouth.

The only time I see any other human beings in person is when I walk Ananda and see someone else walking their dog, or on the rare trips to buy groceries.

I have many meetings for work, and they are all done virtually on my laptop or phone. Sometimes the isolation seems nearly unbearable, but then the worst feelings pass, and I register how fortunate I am, to have a job, to have Ananda, and to have a place to live with a garden that is just beginning to come alive with new flowers and foliage.

Recently I read in the news that Portland police reported an astronomical rise in 911 emergency calls for suicide attempts and suicide threats. Suddenly I felt like I had to find a way to help. My own familiar suicidal feelings were unexpectedly absent. I felt an immense calling to create something that could help people who were struggling to stay alive.

I had an idea about creating a way to use peer support workers who have their own personal experiences dealing with their own behavioral health struggles and who have been extensively trained to help other people. The idea is that these peers could reach out to endangered people by phone, text, and video to give them daily encouragement and contact so that the social isolation would not swallow them up. It would not take the place of the psychiatrists, counselors, therapists, and case managers. It would provide people extra support, every day, so they wouldn't feel so alone.

This is what I have been working on. When I started talking to my co-workers about my idea their reaction was great—they wanted to help create this new program. Suddenly we had a team of people working on this project. I was so surprised, because I usually assume that I have to create things all by myself. But here was a group of people with their various areas of expertise, and we're all coming together to make my idea a reality. Phase 1 will apply to any clients who are extra stressed by the pandemic. Phase 2 will focus on people who are specifically struggling with suicidal feelings.

There is no illusion that this program will solve everything. But if we can just help in some way, then it will be worth it.

I'm working on creating this program during much of the day, but then the isolation of the quarantine for the pandemic slams down on me. I feel exhausted and alone. In the evening, before dark I take Ananda for her walk. Not always, but sometimes we see other people walking their dogs. The rule is we have to stay at least six feet apart so we don't spread the disease, but sometimes Ananda can sniff and wag with the other dog, and this helps make everything better.

Alpine, 1998

Did I really dare to begin a different life—one of hope—or would I just be slammed down like I always had been before? And my new names—Jisho and Ahimsa—would they help guide me?

When it was time for me to begin the clinical trial for the new medication, I had to catch a flight from Portland to Las Vegas, then to Burbank, California, and then I had to get a ride to the huge hospital in Los Angeles. I needed to do this one day a week, for seven weeks, and after that it would happen once every month. The logistics of just getting to the airport in Portland, which was two hours away from Alpine, were daunting, but the pieces fell into place.

My friend Katie from the Zen group picked me up at 3:00 a.m. to drive me to the airport in Portland. I changed planes in Las Vegas, where my senses were overwhelmed because the airport was filled with noisy slot machines. By 10:00 a.m. I was picked up in Burbank by one of the doctors who was working with the clinical trial. I was very surprised to be getting a ride to the hospital from a doctor, but I learned there were a lot of young psychiatrists from other countries who were working with the hospital program until they could get into medical residency training programs in the United States. Many of them were working to improve their fluency in English. Some were from China, Romania, Ukraine or India, and they would practice talking to me in English, and we would have friendly conversations. Once at the hospital there was a routine of blood tests, heart tests, memory tests, movement tests—it seemed like every possible thing got asked, or measured, or examined. The doctor who was in charge of the program was a big, white-haired godly figure with a Scottish brogue; the young psychiatry trainees gathered around him as if he were holy Jesus and they were the disciples waiting to be anointed. When this imposing doctor interviewed me, I could tell that his experience and authority were exceptional, yet his voice with the Scots brogue was soft, and he seemed kind, so I didn't feel too scared of him.

After a few hours at the hospital, all the tests were finished, and a Romanian doctor drove me back to the airport. There were always many hours of waiting at the airport, and then the two different flights back to Portland, and it was midnight when Katie picked me up in her Jeep and took me home to Alpine. This was repeated every week for seven weeks, then once every month. I got to know the routine very well. And I got to know all of the doctors working on the trial. They treated me like I was their "star" patient, and I was happy to be in that role. Every month I had to step on the scale to be weighed, which I dreaded, but every month I had lost weight, so it was always a happy surprise. The voices and hallucinations grew rare.

I thought I would be in the clinical trial for three or four months, but I was informed that the government agency that oversees the development of new medications had decided that much more information was required to see how this drug affected the heart, so the trips to the hospital in Los Angeles were going to last much longer than anyone had expected.

One day I was back in Alpine between my trips to the hospital for the clinical trial, I was out in the yard digging a hole for a new bamboo plant. I dug the hole, carefully placed the bamboo, then packed and smoothed the soil around the base so it was securely planted.

I stood back and looked at the results of my work. *And I had a strange feeling. What was it?*

Suddenly I realized that I was feeling *pleasure*. Pleasure? It had been so long since I had felt pleasure that I had forgotten what it felt like, or that it was even possible. But suddenly I was able to feel it once more, after years of dreary pain, and it was a miraculous gift from the universe. My ability to feel it was helped by taking the new medication. It was profound.

Then I got an inspired Big Idea. I would transform my overgrown yard into a beautiful garden—a verdant refuge. My friend Luma was a Master Gardener, so I asked her to help me. At first, she warned me: it would be an immense amount of work. But my mind was made up—I had to do this. So, with Luma's guidance, I began.

First, a burly neighbor came with a weed whacker and chopped down the tallest grasses, masses of weeds, and vines. When he was finished, it looked like a cyclone had hit. Over the next few weeks I gathered up the various broken plant pieces and put them in what became a huge pile in the farthest corner of the yard. This became my new compost pile. Next, Luma arranged a wonderful, generous gift to me—a gigantic pile of rich black soil was delivered. It sat squarely in the middle of the yard, like a volcanic mountain. It was huge, and if I thought much about what I was going to do with it, I became intimidated, but slowly, I began to fill the wheelbarrow with loads of the precious black substance and took them to different spots where I wanted to have flower beds. I shoveled it out into what became new habitats for growing beautiful things.

It seemed like the pieces were falling magically into place. A man with a backhoe came and dug a big hole beneath the oak tree, just in front of my cabin's back porch. I instructed him to pile the dirt from the hole in front of the base of the oak tree. In time, with the assistance of some friends from the Zen group and others, this hole was turned into a pond that would eventually have koi fish. The pile of dirt at the base of the oak tree became a hill and was covered first with a rubber liner and then with river stones. It all worked so that the water from the pond was pumped up to the top of this hill and then flowed merrily down, back to the bowl of the pond. It made a beautiful sound as it flowed and tumbled over the stones. I quickly learned that I could make this watercourse play different tunes by how I arranged the stones, and I spent hours trying out different arrangements, in quest of the most beautiful melodies. Katie started calling me "Beaver Woman," because I worked with the stones fine-tuning the watercourse like a beaver building its dam.

Luma had a huge garden of her own, and she brought me all sorts of baby plants from her flower beds. We made a special trip north to Washington to a plant nursery that only sold bamboo and came home with her car filled with baby bamboo plants. Bamboo has a special place in my heart, both because it is beautiful, but also because it figures so prominently in Buddhist art. I planted it, seven different varieties, all around the property.

Of course, this took months to do, and at the same time I was making my monthly trips for the clinical trial to get the new medication. The seasons turned and proceeded, and as I felt myself changing, I could look at my yard and see the new plants taking root and putting out new foliage. The bamboo was growing, and in the spring, there were the new flowers—first crocuses, daffodils, then irises, peonies, and more flowers whose names I did not know. Finally, I had saved enough money to go to the store where they sold koi, and I picked out six small fish, each a unique color and personality. One was white with a red circle on his head. I was told that he was special because he looked like the national flag of Japan. I named him Moby, after Moby-Dick, because he was bigger than the others and swam with a bit of a swagger. I named them all, and soon they ate out of my hand when I knelt beside the pond. At night, when I was in bed, I could listen to the sound of the watercourse, and sometimes I would vividly dream that I was underwater, swimming with my koi.

I kept returning to Los Angeles every month. I knew all the doctors by name, and I kept in touch with Lois from the drug company in New York. It was so remarkable because

I didn't have any of the side effects that I had with previous drugs. Every time I got on their scale, I had lost weight. And the voices and frightening sights were simply gone. I didn't feel like the world was hurling itself at me anymore. I would sit out on the back porch with Iris and my friends Katie and Luma, and as I observed the garden and then reflected on the changes in my life, it was clear that a huge transformation was taking place.

One morning I got a call from Lois. She told me that the new medication had finally been approved by the federal agency that oversees these things, which meant that the drug could now be sold in the United States. The clinical trial would end in a few months. I had traveled to Los Angeles every month for more than two years, but now the trips were nearly over. We said goodbye, and I hung up the phone.

I walked out into the yard, beside the koi pond and into my garden. As I looked around me, I realized that this garden was like my life. Both had been overgrown and hopeless, but both had become sources of beauty and vibrant growth.

And now it was time to begin a new phase of growing.

"Human with Lotus"
Pen and ink on paper
30 x 40 in.

FOURTEEN

The guardians were known as dragons,
and were feared by many, thought to be hor-
rendous and violent, but when they came to me
in a dream, I put my arms around their necks—
you can do this in a dream- and we all sang a
little song together in our various voices—
their voices deep and tinged with fire,
my voice a squeaky little peep, then I knew that
we would always love each other and that if I
needed to hide they would welcome me in their
cave—what is fear anyway, except the mistaken
unfamiliarity that shuts our eyes to beauty,
which disappears when our sight is restored?

Portland, 2020

This is the eleventh week of the lockdown for the COVID-19 pandemic. The suffering and unhappiness from the pandemic are huge. But things have gotten much worse. The past few days there have been riots and unrest in many American cities and even in Europe because a Black man named George Floyd was killed by a white police officer who knelt on his neck while he pleaded for his life. The inequities and systemic racism in our country are fully on display. Blacks and Hispanics are also dying of the virus at significantly higher rates than whites. The racism and inequity in America are huge open wounds, and the stress of the pandemic has torn away any scab that might have tried to form. It seems like maybe our society is being torn open so that possibly the problems that we have for so long taken for granted might have a chance to be addressed. Sometimes I can feel a little hope, other times the pain presses down hard.

And all the reports are saying that the rate of suicides is rising. This is true for the clients where I work. I was told that people who have never before contemplated suicide are now considering it. These things fill my mind as I sit on the sofa in my library, where I have everything I need, except for human contact. I am acutely aware that I have everything I need, but so many people have next to nothing, or less. I feel the isolation, and when I walk Ananda every day in the neighborhood, if we see anyone else, it is a relief. I go out of my way to greet them and connect in some even small way. I've also started to carry colored chalk in my pocket so that I can write or draw things on the sidewalk.

I'll write something like "Hang in there!" or "Black Lives Matter," or I'll simply draw a giraffe or some fantastical creature with spots. I know it's not much to write and draw on the sidewalk, but even writing an encouraging message on the sidewalk is a way to do something positive, if even in just a tiny way.

Some days I have just stayed in bed much of the day. Since all of my work meetings are by phone or computer, I figure it doesn't really matter if I get up or not. A few weeks ago, I started to spiral downward, into depression. I wrote my psychiatrist an email, and she called to check on me.

She brought up the question of whether I needed to be in the inpatient psychiatric hospital or some kind of day treatment program. She made a referral for me to get a therapist. In my imagination, as I was lying in bed, I thought about what it would be like to have a plastic bag over my head, suffocating myself. I had not been this low in a long time. I didn't think I wanted to go to the hospital. I need to have Ananda by my side and that wouldn't be possible in the hospital. When I talked to the new therapist, Lacey, it helped a little, but I realized that I was really on my own. I talked to someone from an intensive day treatment program—it was being done online due to the pandemic—but the thought of having any more things I have to do during the day was overwhelming. I have continued meeting online with the team working on creating the virtual peer support program I have envisioned. I realize that I am trying to create the programs that would help me, myself, if they were available. Part of my idea is to make it so that any person who is struggling with suicidal feelings can get support from peer support specialists in addition to their therapist so that they have daily contact, maybe even multiple times a day, with people who understand what they are going through, and who offer understanding and support. Yes, I wish I had this right now. Maybe I can lead the way so it will eventually be available for other people who are struggling like I am.

Last week I had a meeting with the suicide prevention work group up at the medical school. I told them about my digital peer support ideas, and they were receptive. I think a lot of people right now are realizing there is a problem, but no one really knows what to do to really make it better.

Now it is the weekend, thankfully, and I can focus on my painting for the show coming up in June. I'm collaborating with an artist who lives in Mumbai, India. I have been procrastinating working on it, just because I feel so frozen and unable to think about doing much of anything. But I have to get it finished soon—I'm running out of time.

I will call my ninety-five-year-old mother who is having a rough time in the assisted living facility where she lives in San Antonio. She hasn't been able to leave her room in weeks because of the risk of getting the virus. She is not allowed to have visitors or go to visit her friends.

I just hope that she will be able to see her friends again and have pleasure before the end of her life. I can tell that she really doesn't understand the lockdown. She thinks that it is the facility being mean and cheap. I try to call her often to cheer her up, but when I am really depressed myself it is hard to have much to offer her.

It is morning now, and last night there was curfew on Portland streets because of the riots and violence. This is happening all over the country in response to the horrible police murder of George Floyd, in Minneapolis, and other recent police shootings of Black people. Even in some other countries, people are protesting in solidarity with the people here in America who are protesting nightly against the entrenched racism. This level of protest and violence has not happened since the 1960s, during the Civil Rights Movement. This morning I find myself crying hard as I try to make a pot of coffee. The suffering in America and across the entire world is overwhelming,

I am sure I am not the only person crying this morning.

Alpine, 2002
My life suddenly was shining with possibility—could I trust it?

After the clinical trial for the new medication ended, I found myself feeling stronger than I ever had, except maybe when I was ten years old and felt invincible. I took some time to grow stronger in my new recovery. One day I received a call from Lois asking me to speak at a meeting of 1,200 people about my experience of the clinical trial, the new medication, and my healing.

I soon found myself in Orlando, Florida, being transported in a limousine to a fancy hotel, working with a speech writer, and learning how to use a teleprompter. It was surreal. Right before the actual event, I got to meet Lois for the first time. We hugged, so glad to finally meet each other face to face. We had talked on the phone so many times, but we had never met in person. She seemed younger than I had imagined. We entered the huge meeting hall and soon Lois was on the stage, introducing me to the audience. I was surprised by how she told about my persistence and how it had affected her personally and about the story of the clinical trial. Afterwards, as I walked to the stage there was a standing ovation. Then it was my time to speak. I was nervous, but I was ready to do it, and so I dove into my speech. At a few points in my talk, people broke into applause. When the fifteen minutes was over, I received another standing ovation. I was incredulous. It hardly felt real, but I knew it was no hallucination.

I returned to Oregon, back to my life where I was still in treatment at the county mental health program. When I was sitting in the shabby waiting room, waiting for the appointment with my psychiatrist, the contrast between my experience in Orlando giving the speech, and sitting in the depressing health department waiting room was striking. After the usual long wait, I was summoned to my psychiatrist's office. When I was finally sitting across from him, I told him that I had decided that I wanted to get a job and go to work. The recent experience giving the speech had convinced me that I wanted something more than the role of mental patient, and even more importantly, it now seemed like a possibility. When I announced to him that I wanted to get a job, his immediate response was, "You're too sick to work."

I was surprised, but I considered his words. I then decided that I would prove him wrong. With some convincing, he gave me a referral to vocational rehabilitation. They would help me find a job.

Meanwhile, I got another request from the drug company. They wanted to come to my cabin in Alpine and interview me and make a video. It would take half a day and they would pay me to do it. Of course, I agreed. On the appointed day, a team of people from New York City appeared at my door. There was a three-person video crew plus another woman who was in charge of it all. Luma had told me how to cook scones so I could offer them coffee and something to eat when they arrived early that morning. They had lots of technical equipment. First, they set everything up in front of my bookcase next to the door to the pond. The woman in charge asked me questions, and I answered them, basically telling about what my life was like before the clinical trial and how I felt differently now. Sometimes Iris would make noise, barking, sometimes scratching a flea, or her collar would jingle. This meant we would have to stop and start over, but no one suggested that I put Iris out of the room. They seemed to understand that it was important that Iris be there with me. Then we went outside, and they took pictures of me cleaning out the pond with a long pole and walking down the gravel road with Iris. Finally, they took some pictures of the meditation room, with me sitting on the round *zafu* meditation cushion meditating.

It had been easy; it was another adventure—I learned something about how videos are made, and I thought it was actually fun. When it was over, they seemed very happy with the results and went back to New York.

Soon I had another message from the drug company—could I give another speech? I was eager to do it, and it didn't seem very hard, even though this time it was to an audience of psychiatrists in New York City. I simply told the story of how things used to be and how things had changed.

Back in Oregon, I went to "Voc Rehab"—the vocational rehabilitation office. The man assigned to work with me told me that since I was an artist, he thought it would be a good thing for me to get a job in a frame shop, framing other people's art. That didn't appeal to me at all. Nevertheless, he arranged a job interview for me at a local frame shop.

I went to the interview, and the moment I entered the shop I was struck by what a depressing environment it was. The idea of working there, framing other people's art, seemed incredibly bleak.

I was certain this was not what I wanted to do. I wanted to do something more like the work I was doing occasionally with the drug company. At first Voc Rehab resisted my idea, but eventually they gave in and assigned a woman to work with me to make it happen.

Every day I would take Iris for a long walk up steep Green Peak Road. We took this walk in every kind of weather. There were fields of sheep, both white and black, gray and white llamas, vineyards, and places where the road went through tunnels of thick evergreen forest. When we finally got to the top, where there was a little cabin, and we looked out across the world and marveled at the beauty, I felt so much gratitude.

One day I got the idea that I would see if I could teach some drawing classes to clients at the mental health program in Corvallis where I was still seeing my therapist and my psychiatrist—the same one who had told me I was too sick to work. I wrote up a proposal and asked the receptionist to give it to Pat, the person in charge. I knew her from my many years of being a patient. I had often seen her as a stern impediment to whatever it was that I wanted to do, like once when I didn't like my therapist and wanted to switch to a new one. Anytime I asked her about anything, she always had said no. No, no, no. One time, when I was in the day treatment program, I had dumped all the contents of my pill bottles—dozens of pills—on the floor, in protest of something she had said no to me about. Another time I had refused to sign the copy of the treatment plan that my therapist had composed for me without using any of my own ideas. Pat told me to sign it, but I refused. Later I learned that my refusal to sign had created a big problem for them because it violated an official state requirement. The plan was their plan, it had nothing to do with my own goals or personal thoughts or ideas, so I was not going to endorse it. I was used to pushing back on whatever Pat wanted me to do. But here I was with a new idea, and I was cautiously hopeful.

The day after Pat received my proposal, she called and said she had a counterproposal for me. There was going to be a five-county art show for mental health consumers on the coast and she wondered if I would be the liaison for our county's part in it? I was totally surprised by the idea because it was unlike anything I had ever done before, and also it seemed like Pat was giving me a chance to do some positive. I immediately accepted. I started visiting all the groups and organizations where mental health clients met, and I encouraged them to make art for the show. I was so stressed by doing this, but I totally threw myself into the work. The agreement was that I would work twelve hours a week, but it consumed me, and I worked many more hours. I did everything I could think of to get people to make art, so the art show would be a success. One local group I visited to encourage participation was a small group of mental health consumers called BEARS, which stood for "Band of Empowered Advocates Reclaiming Self-determination." I thought this was the best acronym I had ever heard. There were really only about four or five persons in this organization, but they were passionate about getting together and exchanging ideas about how to improve the mental health system. They had big ideas, and their discussions were animated and ambitious. I visited them a few times, to talk up the art show, and then they told me they had received a grant to create a peer-delivered services training program for the county. They told me they wanted to hire me to be the project's coordinator. But how could I possibly do this? I was still working on the art show and sometimes giving speeches for the drug company, plus I knew nothing about this thing called "peer-delivered services." And most of all, I didn't know anything about how to be a coordinator for a grant. All of this was totally outside the experience of anything I had ever done. I thought it was nice that they wanted me to do it, but I was clear that I didn't have the knowledge or qualifications.

The art show got closer, and I had collected more pieces of art from our county than there had ever been before. With Pat's blessing I assembled a group of mental health clients one weekend, and on the floor of the waiting room at the health department, we painted a huge mural together. It was bright and joyful, based on Matisse's painting "The Dance." There were about a dozen of us who were clients of the county mental health program. With the radio blasting rock and roll, we all worked together. I had created the overall design.

The background was in blues, magenta, and greens. For the foreground each person had taken a white piece of canvas cut to look like a human shape, and on it they wrote very personal responses to a list of questions I had compiled, like what was their favorite musical instrument, or what gave them the greatest pleasure, and where was their favorite place. Each canvas human figure was totally unique.

Later, after the brightly painted background was dry, I glued the human figures to it and painted a thick gold line that joined them all together in a circle. It was dazzling. A picture was taken, and it appeared in the local newspaper.

The day before the art show, I was in New York City giving another speech. After the event was over, I flew right back to Portland. The drug company arranged for a black limousine to drive me all the way to Newport, the city on the coast where the art show was being held. It was a long way, and the limo driver got a pillow out of the trunk so I could put my head down and sleep. When I arrived at the show, the sight was stunning. The work we had collected from dozens of mental health consumers from our county was profuse, much more than any of the other counties. It overflowed the space, and then there was our glorious mural. This was a real victory. I was told that this was the biggest success ever in the history of the show. Having so much success was an incredible, new experience. I was thrilled and could barely believe it. But I had to believe it—it was no illusion or fiction. It was real.

I wasn't so sure about the next step though. I had changed my mind and with trepidation, I was going to be the coordinator for the BEARS peer service grant project. What did this mean? I certainly didn't know, but I had a new sense of confidence, not entirely steady, but I was doing things I never had guessed would be possible.

I had a sense that the story of my life had gone in a whole new direction. In my mind I told myself I was "in the lap of the Universe." This was the only way I could explain it to myself. It meant that I was safe and that the Universe was in charge, not me.

"Untitled (Person with Celtic Lion)"
Pen and ink on paper
30 x 40 in.

FIFTEEN

All that you dread, all that is repulsive,
all that is horrendous—don't these ideas
deserve a line or two, among all the other
sentences that reach for sunlight and nobility—
when it is finally over, I will ask myself if I
have really paid attention, have I held it all—
isn't it all really beautiful, when the wind
moves rapidly, passionately, through
the branches of the trees.

Portland, 2020

I just got an alert on my phone that Portland is under overnight curfew again, from 8:00 tonight until 6:00 a.m. tomorrow. I had a Zoom online meeting with some other artists, and we shared what we are working on. Now I needed to take Ananda for her walk before it got too late.

On our walk, I saw my neighbor Sunny working in her yard, pulling weeds. She said she was going to a Black Lives Matter protest tonight at 6:00 at Laurelhurst Park, which isn't too far away.

I would like to go, but I don't want to go alone, and the logistics of getting there and getting back are more than I can handle today. On our walk, I wrote on the sidewalk in chalk "Kindness not Violence," and I drew some bird shapes that were supposed to be doves. This is what I can do right now. It isn't much, but it is what I can do.

Last week I got into an online discussion about the use of language when discussing suicide. Many people now agree that it is not skillful to say "commit" suicide, since it evokes committing a crime, which suicide is not. In a post on a suicide prevention listserv, someone used the phrase "combat suicide." I wrote a response saying it would be better not to use the term "combat" when talking about preventing suicide because it evokes war and violence. I was completely surprised by how many people wrote responses back. Some people agreed with me and thanked me, and some people disagreed.

One person wrote that it wasn't any different than when he talks about "fighting his demons."

Someone else said they were encouraging people who are suicidal to "battle suicide."

I thought more about the idea of fighting with one's demons and waging battles. This is a predominantly Christian culture. In the Christian religion, the devil is seen as the enemy, to be vanquished, or destroyed. Demons are aligned with the devil. I think that when people talk about their demons, they are usually referring to some part of themselves that hurts, that is in pain. They objectify that part of themselves that hurts and call it a demon or see it as some kind of enemy to be gotten rid of. When we have pain, I think it is more likely to be helpful if we treat that pain with kindness and comfort. If I fight that demon, which is really my own pain objectified, then it isn't too big of a stretch to think of getting a gun and killing it. Kill that demon. Kill the devil. Since the pandemic has been happening, it is reported that gun sales have skyrocketed—a bigger increase in sales than ever seen before. I know the level of collective and personal pain in our society and world is enormous right now. With all this extra pain, don't we really need more comfort and tenderness? Not more guns. Not more killing. I can tell that my own pain level has increased lately.

If I push on my pain, as to get rid of it, then doesn't it just push back? But even knowing this, a few nights ago I was daydreaming about putting the plastic bag over my head and suffocating myself. It seemed desirable to just exit this earthly predicament. Now I can see more clearly that what I really need is connection and caring from people. Even just connecting with the other artists on the online Zoom meeting this afternoon helped ease my pain.

I guess it is inconsistent for me to think about putting a plastic bag over my head one day, and then a few days later to argue against using violent language. But this is how it really is. This is the irony and contrast of my life. The problem of having painful feelings is not gone. Sometimes I am overwhelmed by them. But now I am usually able to step back before I am totally swallowed up. I am able to feel empathy for others who are struggling and talking about "fighting with their demons" and to encourage them to hang on to their lives. And I know, from firsthand experience, that the way to hang on is to somehow make room in one's self for some sort of comfort, and gentleness.

Do I always do this?

No, at least not at first. But it more often occurs to me to connect somehow with someone who will show me the kindness I need, especially when I find it impossible to summon up the caring for myself on my own.

But about violence—and the huge pain being caused by the racism in our society, and really all humanity suffering in this pandemic, in the inequities—there is just so much pain—and it is no surprise that there is so much violence right now. And the current president of the United States is encouraging the violence. For many people it is the only known way of responding to pain. Do we dare even to hope that there will come a greater wisdom and capacity for kindness in the face of the pain of these times? The idea of hope—I now remember the German artist Gerhard Richter's words: "Art is the highest form of hope." I don't think that art is the solution to everything, but suddenly I am very glad to be part of the art show coming up in a few weeks, where artists from across the world have collaborated to create something beautiful. This gives me hope, and maybe it will help bring hope to others as well.

It is evening now. I was just sitting in my library writing this story when I heard the sounds of shouting voices and pounding of drums. After a few minutes I got curious and went out the front door to see what it was about. At the corner, very close, walking down Sixtieth Avenue was a long procession of hundreds of protesters. I went out and stood by the curb. They were shouting slogans about "Black Lives Matter," "Hands Up, Don't Shoot!" and "Say His Name—George Floyd!" I didn't have a banner or a sign, but I raised my arms as high as I could and formed peace signs with each of my hands. I tried to chant along with the protesters, but tears poured down my face, and I could only cry. I held my hands high like that until they had all passed. I was so grateful to the protesters and so grateful to have the opportunity to stand with them.

Meghan J.M. Caughey

Most of them were young. Some of them saw my peace signs and flashed the same back to me. I am still weeping. Maybe there is hope.

I just had an email from Billie. I had not heard from her in several months. She said that Tim had left town when the quarantine began, and she didn't know where he had gone. She is worried about him and really having a hard time with the isolation of the quarantine. I could relate to her feelings about the isolation. I can understand about her worry about Tim, and her missing him, but at the same time I wonder if it might be better for her to move on from that relationship.

I don't say this to her—it is up to her to make this decision, but I understand her loneliness. I will make an effort to check on her more often and hopefully we can be more closely connected, even if it's not in person but through texts and phone calls. I think it would help us both.

Corvallis, 2006

What was this new world? Did I belong here?

Now I had a new job as the coordinator for a grant with the BEARS organization. I didn't even really know exactly what "peer support" or "peer-delivered services" was about. I soon found out: It's when people diagnosed with their own behavioral health issues reach a level of personal healing, and then get intensive training so they can help other people who are referred to as their "peers." The idea is that we who have gone through rough mental health times ourselves are often more able to empathize and connect with other people who are struggling. Because of this shared connection, we can be very effective in understanding and having empathy. It's all about sharing in the healing process. In some ways this is a radical idea, because most often the idea has been that only doctors, and other trained professional people like nurses, therapists and social workers, could be effective in helping people who are considered sick. But in recent years there has been a growing understanding that having "gone through the fire" can be an asset when trying to help other people make it through their own fires.

This is what happened in 1935 with Bill W. who founded Alcoholics Anonymous. His own experience became the necessary ingredient that has made the AA movement so effective. He started something new and profound, and the people who themselves struggled with addiction powerfully supported others to become sober. Over the years it morphed and spread, and the whole concept of peer support gained legitimacy.

Part of that process has been that the experience of having a mental illness or addiction has begun to be viewed as a possible source of valuable knowledge and wisdom. This is still a radical idea in most of the culture. A person's mental illness becomes a strength—what a concept! And many of us don't even use the term *mental illness*. We would prefer to say "mental health challenges" or use some other nonmedical description.

My new job was to study examples of peer support from all over the country and figure out what works best so we could replicate it. I immersed myself in this new world. I learned that there was a peer support training in Portland, and I made trips to visit it and study it. Slowly, by studying groups all over the country and talking to lots of different people, I started to put together a model where trained peer support workers would practice mutuality and compassion, and how powerful it is when people with similar experiences connect with each other in the quest of healing their pain. I worked with the other BEARS members for weeks, and we finally had created a detailed representation of what our peer support training program could ideally look like. Finally, we were able to finish organizing it and get it typed up into an official document; the goal of the grant was accomplished.

Occasionally during this time, I would go to some other city and give a speech for the drug company. On one trip they sent me to a hotel in San Francisco where I spent a day learning about how to speak publicly from an expert media trainer. I had never heard of this before, but apparently she had even trained the royal family in Saudi Arabia—so now it was my turn. I had to give a speech that I had prepared for her. It was filmed, then she analyzed it with me, and told me how to do it better. I wasn't nervous at first, but then I had to give the speech again, still being filmed, while using all the new ideas she had told me to use. This second time I was really tense, my confidence was totally missing, and so I struggled, but I still did it. By the end of the day I had learned some important new things about giving speeches, and it would never be the same after this.

As the grant ended, one of the BEARS members, a woman named Terry, and I went to Eastern Oregon for a weeklong training to become certified as peer mentors. At the end of the long week of training in things like listening skills, person-driven plans, and various support skills, we were given certificates of completion. Now that I had this certificate, I decided to apply for a job in Eugene at a mental health program called Pathways, where they taught classes and groups for people who had mental health challenges. I went to the job interview, and the next day they offered me the job. I had a sense of confidence because I was "in the lap of the Universe." Suddenly I found myself with a "real" job. I was hired to be a peer mentor. It was just for 23 hours a week even though I wanted to work full time. They wouldn't hire me full time because it would mean they would have to pay for me to have health insurance, which was necessary for full-time employees. I needed health insurance, since it was necessary for me to regularly visit a psychiatrist, but I was in a common predicament of not having health care through my work and soon not qualifying for the public health system, which I had received when I was considered to be disabled. Still, I was determined to work. I would have to trust "the Universe" to figure this out.

The Pathways program was mostly classes and groups for people who had a behavioral health diagnosis, like me. In some ways it nearly seemed more like a community college than a treatment program. There was a yoga class at noon for clients and staff. Sometimes I would lead it if the regular teacher was absent. Mostly I led different types of groups, wrote many treatment notes, and just hung out and chatted with the people, my peers, who were enrolled in the program.

One of the clients was a very tall man in his thirties named Robert who had schizophrenia, just like me. He had a long snarled black beard and flashing dark eyes beneath bushy, black eyebrows. He would walk through the building dragging a big noisy bag of empty soda cans, mumbling to himself, and when he passed anyone in the hall, he would grumble extra loud. Because he was so tall and so noisy, people were afraid of him. People always moved away when they saw him coming; no one really ever tried to talk to him. He was tolerated, but mostly left out of things happening. I observed this phenomenon and thought that it was isolating for Robert and that the dynamic didn't seem to benefit anyone, most of all Robert. And I was curious about him as a person.

I decided to talk to him. I approached him in the hall and asked if we could talk. He grumbled a "yes." We started a conversation and eventually, much to my surprise and pleasure, he told me a joke about an ostrich and a tiger who went on a date. I'm not sure if it even really had a punch line, but it was still really funny, and we started laughing together. I don't know many jokes, but I told him my standard joke about the bartender asking the horse, "Hey, buddy, why the long face?" It is the only joke I know, but we both were soon in stitches, laughing together. It was such a wonderful surprise.

Eventually I asked if I could tell him something serious, and he said yes. I shared with him that sometimes, the way he acted—making noise with the bag of cans, talking to himself and making other vocal sounds—was scary to some of the other people. He stood there listening with full attention. I gently suggested that it would be better to hold the bag of cans in his hands, so they didn't clang, and then to say "hello" to people instead of grumbling to himself. I knew this wasn't a simple thing, but I was certain he was capable of doing this because of how, when I was at the Cathexis Program, years ago, I had seen how people diagnosed with schizophrenia could learn to act in nonstereotypical ways so that they fit in better with other people. I was sure that no one else at Pathways thought anything different was possible for Robert, but once I explained to him which actions were scaring other people, he seemed to understand. We practiced together how to say hello in an unscary way. It was a new idea for him. He obviously didn't mean to scare people. He understood what it was like to be scared, and he didn't want to cause it. He just didn't know what to do differently. I gave him a few ideas—like saying "Hi, how are you," not standing right over people, not clanging the cans—and he understood. It was obvious that he was motivated to try it. After that, with some coaching and role playing, he usually was much more approachable and no longer scary. Occasionally I would need to remind him to not hover right over another person because it might scare them, and he would remember and seemed glad for the input. I tried to find a daily joke to share with him, and we would delight in laughing together, even when the joke was pretty lame. It was always fun to joke around with him and laugh together.

Other people had just assumed that he would always be "Scary Robert, the Schizophrenic" and that he could not be expected to do anything different. They didn't have positive expectations for him. But he actually had lots of potential and was motivated to fit in with people. He just needed friendly feedback and people to believe he could do something different. When he started acting differently, people started to respond to him in a more positive way. He became a real member of the community like everyone else. Many people in society and medicine give up on people who have serious challenges like schizophrenia. I want to say that so much more is possible than most people realize or expect. Schizophrenia or other mental illnesses should not be a death sentence. Everyone deserves better, and it starts with creating an opening for new possibilities with positive expectations based on people's strengths and the need for connection.

I had been working at Pathways for about four months. It was 2006. There was a staff meeting, and the topic was an important new study that had just been released. This landmark study said that people who have serious mental illness die on average twenty-five years earlier than the general population. When I heard this, I sat upright, and a shot of adrenaline flooded through me. A huge percentage of the deaths were due to preventable causes including lifestyle factors—like smoking, diabetes, and suicide. In just the four months I had been working there, I personally knew of four of our clients who had tragically died prematurely. This study confirmed what I had seen. It was true. And shocking. I felt like someone had just punched me in the gut.

As I sat there, I felt the growing realization that I needed to do something personally to change this. I made a vow to myself that I would dedicate my work to changing this awful statistic. We all deserve to live, whether or not we have mental illness.

In the following week I designed a new group to share with the clients. I used things that were personally helpful to me, like mindfulness and wellness plans, and I called it the LOTUS Group. LOTUS is an acronym I created to mean "Lifestyles Overcoming Trouble Using Support." It was an awkward name in one way, but the big idea was that we would use the mud of our lives to support our lives blossoming into beautiful flowers—the same idea underlying my paintings.

The group got started with about six or seven clients, plus me. We practiced mindfulness and shared about our lifestyle goals. One man wanted to stop smoking. I had no idea of what he could do to accomplish his goal. Finally, we got the idea that he would attend a knitting group because if he learned to knit then maybe it would help give his hands something different to do besides holding a cigarette. We met every week to check in with one another on our progress toward our goals. We always began with our mindfulness practice. And we talked about our goals. The members of the group started to grow close and encouraged one another. The sense of mutual support grew strong. The man who was trying to stop smoking reported smoking a few less cigarettes each week. People became invested in one another's successes. I was excited by our collective growth. This group could not solve everything, but it was a tangible way to address the terrible statistic of people dying so early. And it brought us together.

I became convinced that this was worth sharing with other mental health programs. There was going to be a big national conference in Washington, D.C., about mental health. I got a scholarship to attend and when I was there, I told everyone who would listen about the LOTUS Group and how I wanted to spread it everywhere. When I had a chance to talk to the president of the organization, he encouraged me to go back and grow the group in Oregon first before trying to tackle the nation. OK, I would do that.

When I got back to Oregon, I went to a meeting with all the directors of mental health programs from across the state. I explained to them how the LOTUS Group was a way for those of us who have mental health challenges to support each other and help change the reality of premature death. One of the people at the meeting was the director of the county health program where I was a client. A few days later I got an unexpected call from him. He asked if I would come work for the county health department and start a LOTUS program there. He said he would create a full-time position for me as peer wellness coordinator, and it would be my job to start a program like what I had designed while working on the grant with BEARS. I jumped into it immediately. Here was the offer of a real, full-time job, doing something that I really cared about. And it even meant I would have health insurance. I was struck by the happy irony that the psychiatrist who had once told me that I was "too sick to work" was now going to be my work colleague. Here I was, fifty years old, and I was going to have a full-time job for the first time in my life! Even my mother had written off the possibility that I would ever be able to work and not be supported by government assistance and food stamps. Now, it seemed like my life was just beginning. From my position, I was "in the lap of the Universe," and I was filled with hope and enthusiasm.

"White Wind Lotus"
Oil on canvas
9 x 12 in.

SIXTEEN

Trying to Make Art during These Times

Why is it so impossible to pick up my paint brush?
canvas pleads with me for attention
"Give me life! Let me matter!"
but I am frozen into the hard shape
of a woman sitting
on the sofa, it is morning
a half cup of coffee
sun comes in sideways through the blinds
But somehow it seems
like the world is now dead
there is nothing, no reason
to express, or describe, or strive
for beauty, or
meaning
Has my heart died
or is it just stillborn
will it ever awaken from this
terrible, raw dream?
I have no answer, but perhaps
when the light moves
across the room into
afternoon
I will find an urge of gesture

and the cadmium red mark
will finally be born.

Portland, 2020

In the middle of this pandemic, and the pain of racism and hope for change here in the United States, there is something remarkable happening, based on art. A local gallery has commissioned thirty artists from around the world and teamed us up into pairs. We are now part of a show called "The View from Here." Part of the idea is to show how the world pandemic cannot stop people from coming together—actually, it is even more of a reason to connect. The artist I am paired with is Aravind Deep Sing, a twenty-three-year-old artist in Mumbai, India. Aravind and I connected on both Zoom and Instagram.

When we first talked together, we pondered the overall theme for our collaboration, and I asked him about his favorite idea. He immediately responded, "Love." I thought this was a great idea.

Our work is a shared expression of love, along with our rich conversations where we share stories about our lives. I feel like we are 100 percent genuine with each other. The cultures of India and the United States have different traditions that try to dictate how love can be expressed. We prove that art goes beyond these walls.

There is a twelve-and-a-half-hour time difference between Portland and Mumbai. Sometimes when I'm awake at 2:00 a.m. or 3:00 a.m., I call him up using my laptop, and we have rich, long conversations deep into the night until morning. We share stories about our lives, and about what and who we love, and stories about the truest loves of our lives. I told him about marrying Kent, and how it was so important to me that our ceremony showed that I wasn't owned by any man, and how at our wedding, no one owned me or could "give me away." I described how our passion has not died even though the years have passed and we have divorced. He told me about the great love he shared with one of his teachers who was much older than him. I sense that now he might be caught in the middle of his parents' expectations of a traditional arranged marriage, even with his own intense nonconforming passions.

We tell each other our own sacred life stories and listen to each other with no hint of judgment.

I wrote a poem for him:

For Aravind in Mumbai

Our wings fly and sing together
across the edges of the globe
it matters not that forty years lie between
parameters of our lives
2 AM, I call you
twelve and a half hours
really not so much
in the eyes of the timeless universe
you are an old soul
even so young
and me, I am old
though also young
deep within the bones of our images
the years dissolve into vibrant tubes of oil paint
sticks of blackest charcoal
our language of art
we talk through the night

ribs of our loves shared freely
not to be impeded
unlikely, unstoppable,
cadmium red painted passions
unite us, a shared expression
the stars and moon
watch over us both
finally, I'm able
to get back to sleep
as it becomes dawn.

I was supposed to take the finished painting to the gallery this afternoon, but I decided I needed to paint the edges of the canvas black, instead of gray. I called the gallery and spoke to the director, who asked how it was working with Aravind. As I told him the story of our calls and conversations, I realized I need to write about the process so it can be part of the official catalog for the show.

I just finished painting the edges of the canvas black, mixed with special liquid concoctions that will hurry up the drying time of the oil. Hopefully, the painting will be dry enough so I can deliver it tomorrow afternoon. Suddenly this art show has become very important to me. There is so much death and pain around me, but here is beauty and connection. I must admit I feel love for Aravind—a love that is undeniable, but impossible at once. We are so far apart in age and geography, yet here we are, so able to communicate about the really important things and we seem to understand each other so well. We share passion. We share art.

In the middle of this pandemic, and all the social unrest and pain, here is love and creation. At this moment, this project fills me with wonder and hope.

Corvallis, 2008

Who was this person who was supposed to be me?

I was now working full time in a brand-new job at the county health department. Because my previous psychiatrist was now my work colleague, I needed a new psychiatrist who could prescribe my essential psych medication. The big problem was that in Corvallis, there were no psychiatrists who were taking new patients. I got on a six-month waiting list to see a woman shrink, but until then I would need to go to the emergency department of the local hospital and see whatever doctor was on call whenever I needed a medication prescription or refill.

On one of these trips, I sat across the examination room from a doctor whom I had never seen before, and I tried to explain to him why I needed my usual, specific medication. I confessed to him that sometimes I was struggling in my new role of full-time employee, even though it was actually going surprisingly well. He didn't accept my report. Earlier he had consulted the hospital records about me, so many endless pages, which were full of the terrible accounts of my years of hospitalizations, overdoses, suicide attempts, extreme nightmares—overall very bad times.

He had his own idea of what medication I should take. He told me what he was going to prescribe. I objected—I didn't agree with him and wasn't going to take something simply because he thought it was a good idea. I knew what I needed and felt the decision was mine, not his. I communicated this to him very plainly, politely, but with no apology. I knew that I was the expert here, not him. His response was that if I did not do what he said and take the medication he wanted me to take, then he would involuntarily hospitalize me in the psychiatric inpatient unit. I was utterly shocked.

I had just gone through an official state training about the Oregon laws that govern how people can be involuntarily committed or hospitalized in psychiatric inpatient units. Based on my recent official professional eight-hour training, I knew that there was no way that I met the legal criteria for him to do this to me.

But there I was, in the role of patient, and he was in the powerful role of doctor. He could break all the rules and the law, and at this moment I had absolutely no recourse. He was coercing me, and because I didn't want to be hospitalized, I would have to abandon my own wishes and opinions and tell him I would do what he wanted. I was angry, scared—but more than anything, I was shocked. And I certainly didn't want to be hospitalized. I thought to myself that here was an example of a failing mental health system, and I was determined to work to fix it. I took the unwanted bottle of pills and left. When I got home, I threw the pills in the garbage mixed with some coffee grounds.

I wrote a grant and was awarded funding to start the county health department's peer wellness program. I led LOTUS Groups and designed a peer wellness specialist training program.

Pat was my supervisor now. One day she called me into her office with a special assignment. A family on the East Coast had contacted the health department because they were concerned about their sister who was homeless, had schizophrenia, and refused any kind of mental health treatment. The woman's name was Chrissy Lake, and she was apparently living in her ancient maroon Buick, which she parked on the streets of Corvallis. The family was very worried about her because they had not heard from her in months. They wanted to make sure she was safe and to help her get into stable housing. They loved her but had no way to find her or help her. Pat gave me a blurred photocopy of a picture of her face and her Buick's license plate number and asked me to see if I could find her. We would try to help.

I studied the photo and then began to drive around Corvallis looking for her old, maroon Buick. It was fall and the Oregon rains had begun. I drove up and down through the downtown streets, along the river, and then through the various neighborhoods. I did this day after day, but there was no sign of her. There was a soup kitchen in town in the basement of a church. I kept an outfit of old clothes in my car trunk, and after work I would change out of my work clothes into frayed jeans and an ancient fuzzy gray oversized hoodie with a big hole in one sleeve. I would stand in the line of homeless diners patiently waiting to be served dinner by kind volunteers, all the while looking for Chrissy Lake. I did this for weeks.

Then one night, when it was late and the soup kitchen was about to close, a woman came through the door in a tan trench coat. Her coat was soiled and worn, but obviously a quality brand. Under her arm she had a tall stack of books. The minute I saw her I knew it was Chrissy Lake. I took my tray and went to a table and sat down. I watched her go through the line, get her tray, and then go and sit down at an empty table in the very back of the room. After a few minutes I quietly took my tray and went to her table.

"Mind if I sit?" I asked softly.

"Sure," she replied in a near whisper, not looking up.

I sat down and started to eat. Finally, I made a small comment on her stack of books. I asked her what they were about. She started to explain about how one of them was about a distant relative of hers who was a famous person in England in the 1700s. I listened and eventually we began a tentative conversation. When it seemed like we were sufficiently connected, I decided I should disclose to her about how I worked at the health department. First, I handed her my business card, but not for my job as county peer wellness coordinator. Instead, I gave her the card with my name, art website address, and the phrase "Art is Essential for Life." It had a red Chinese symbol, called a "chop," that said the word *freedom*. I had the stone chop made with the red symbol once when I had been in San Francisco's Chinatown on the first anniversary of the historic uprising in Tiananmen Square. I had chosen the word *freedom* because of how I had been tied down in restraints in seclusion rooms so many times when I had been hospitalized. Being free means something very real and tangible to me; I do not take it for granted.

Chrissy Lake took the card and looked at it. She asked me if I was an artist. Yes, I replied simply. I paused, but then I explained how I also had a job at the county health department and that her family was worried about her and hoped to find her so maybe they could pay for her to stay in a hotel instead of in her car on the streets. I told her I could help get her a room in a hotel, if she wanted it. She listened, but only shook her head "no." I didn't try to push or convince her. I sensed I should leave her alone, but I did ask if I could sit with her again sometime if we happened to see each other at the soup kitchen. She said yes. Then I left.

Several weeks later, after work, I went back to the soup kitchen. This time I didn't change into my old "soup kitchen" clothes; I left on my professional gray jacket, trousers, and short black leather boots. I figured from the look of her trench coat that she might be comfortable with more stylish clothes. Again, right before the doors closed for the night, Chrissy Lake came in, wearing her tan trench coat. Our eyes met, and once she had her tray, she came and sat at my otherwise empty table. Except for a modest greeting, we didn't try to make conversation. Somehow it seemed OK to just sit quietly together. When it came time to leave, we bid each other good night, got up, and went in our separate directions. I saw her once after that, and again we just sat together, but didn't try to converse too much. I didn't bring up the idea of her staying in a hotel again. I simply tried to communicate acceptance and respect, which I genuinely felt.

After that night I did not see her for many weeks.

I had to go to Washington, D.C., for another mental health conference where I was to give a presentation on my work about peer support services. On the final night of the conference I got an email from Pat on my phone. All it said was that police had found Chrissy Lake dead in her car that morning. She apparently had gotten wet in a sudden rainstorm and died in the night from hypothermia.

How could this be? No!!!! I sobbed and sobbed. There was no one I could go to for support.

There I was, alone in Washington, D.C., and Chrissy Lake was dead. All I could do was cry.

The next day, coming back to Oregon on the airplane, I just sat and cried during the whole trip. There was nothing else I could do.

She was gone. I would never see her again.

Later in the week, her brother and two sisters came from the East Coast to Corvallis. I met them on the front steps of the public library where Chrissy had spent so much of her time. In the large reading room with the tall ceilings and comfortable upholstered armchairs I told them, "This was Chrissy's living room." Then we went to the park across the street where there was a lush rose garden, and I said, "This was Chrissy's garden."

Next we went to the church beside to the park, down the steps to the basement where the soup kitchen happened every night, and I said, "This was Chrissy's dining room." The following day there was a small memorial service for Chrissy Lake in the chapel. When I walked into the sacred space, I looked at the walls, and I was shocked to see they were covered with huge, lush oil paintings. Beautifully painted landscapes. Lush flowers. Vast hillsides covered with sheep. Chrissy Lake had been a talented painter. Yet, I had no clue of this before now. She had never even mentioned it. I thought back about our first meeting and how I had first given her my card that said, "Art is Essential for Life." Probably the only reason she tolerated contact with me was because I was also an artist. And she probably understood about art being essential for life.

I was filled with grief, but also with a sense of wonder at the mystery of it all.

One day, after nearly four years in my county job, I had a message from a big mental health nonprofit organization in Portland. There were considered a "safety net" organization, which meant they were there for the people who were poor and who were on government insurance like Medicaid, and who would otherwise just "fall through the cracks." The CEO and chief medical officer wanted to meet with me. I met them at the lunchroom in the basement of the state Capitol after we had earlier been on the Capitol steps to lobby for some mental health legislation that would help our people. The chief medical officer was named Maggie. After a very long, far-ranging conversation, they invited me to come to Portland to work for their organization and build a peer wellness program there. They would create a senior director position for me. I knew right away that I wanted to do it. I said yes. It meant I would have to leave my house among the Christmas tree farms with the koi pond and move to the big city of Portland. I surprisingly felt ready to do it. It seemed right. I had never thought I would want to live in a big city, but now it seemed like it was time and would be a grand adventure.

"Holding on to a Hard Landscape"
Pen and ink on paper
10 x 12 in.

SEVENTEEN

When?

How do we make this world
can it hold more tears
what can I offer you, Child
is there some fine
belief
a dazzling free fantasy
would you even believe it if
I held it in my hand
offering it freely
to you only
to your tribe
only
hold tight to life
dear soul
the fires rage now
but soon the autumn rains
will flow down upon
our heads
eventually our masks
will be removed.

Portland, 2011

I t seemed like I had done the impossible thing—escaped from the diagnosis of schizophrenia—but had I really? I wasn't really sure, but I would give it everything I had inside me.

I moved to Portland and began the work of starting a new peer-delivered services program. I trained people who had recovered from their own struggles with mental health challenges, sometimes combined with addiction, homelessness, and incarceration. I adapted to big city life surprisingly well, and my service dog, Ananda, loved to go to the office with me every day. Everyone there adored her, and when anyone came to my office, there was a ritual where she did a trick and they had to reward her with a dog biscuit from a big jar I kept on a shelf on my bookcase.

For the first time, I started having long phone conversations with my brother Lance, who lived in a double-wide trailer in rural Georgia. He had been a captain in the Army in Vietnam and later had served in Iraq. He was ten years older than me, and when we were growing up, I idolized him. He had taught me how to walk in the woods without making a sound, so we didn't scare the animals, and he always carried a snake stick in case we encountered a copperhead. When I was six years old, he taught me how to shoot a rifle in the backyard. Eventually we grew older, and he went off to college, and then to war in Vietnam. I hardly ever saw or had any contact with him after that. He had gone to war, and I eventually started having my mental health problems and getting hospitalized. I never heard anything from him. He was absent. I would sometimes wonder why he never checked on me when I was having such a hard time. But I just accepted it and thought it was a sign of the dysfunction of my family.

When I was in Portland, in my new job, I got word that he had diabetes. I was the only one in the family who knew anything about health care, or how to research things on the computer. I started sending him and his wife, a Korean woman named So, information about what foods he should eat and recipes for diabetics. He and I started to talk regularly on the phone together. His health continued to deteriorate, and he had a small stroke—a TIA, or transient ischemic attack. Our conversations grew longer, and he began to tell me stories about his Vietnam War experience. It seemed like he needed to talk about these times to purge them from his mind. He described carrying an injured German shepherd war dog named King on his shoulders for miles to get help after a battle. There was a very gruesome story of how, after an ambush and battle, he had to walk among the ruins and debris and pick up his dead men's body parts and put them in plastic bags to send to their families back in the States. Another time he had shot and killed a Vietnamese woman who was running toward him with a grenade.

He spewed these terrible stories with an intensity; it seemed like he had never told them to anyone before, and now he had to expel them from his psyche, where they had been locked up for so many years. All I could do was listen. It now made sense why he had never called to check on me for decades. His own pain had totally consumed him, and he had no capacity to add my pain to his. At one point he told me that someday when he died, he wanted to be buried at Andersonville National Cemetery in Georgia. During the Civil War, Andersonville was the site of a Confederate prisoner of war camp where many atrocities had been committed. Thirteen thousand Union soldiers had died there on the putrid soil with the diseased creek. After the war, it became a national cemetery for the thousands of dead soldiers from many different wars. When my own father had died, Lance had him buried there, and he felt like he had done something very respectful and significant for our father. It was an honor to be buried there, and it was what Lance said he wanted someday for himself. When he told me this, I didn't say much; I just figured he was getting in touch with his eventual mortality and had happened to mention it to me offhandedly. I stored it in the back of my mind.

In October I called him on his birthday, but he didn't seem to want to talk very much.

A few weeks later I got the news that he had had a major stroke. After a few weeks in the hospital, he was taken home. He couldn't move much or do much to take care of himself. Out of necessity, his wife changed his used diapers. One day, when his wife had briefly left him so she could go to the pharmacy, he managed to drag himself out into the yard and shot himself in the chest with the largest handgun made. I got the call that he was dying, and soon he was dead. Quickly the family made plans for his cremation and burial. The first plan was to bury him in the cemetery of the nearby military base, but I made sure he was buried in Andersonville National Cemetery. No one else had known he wanted this. I was grateful that he had told me this wish, so I could make sure it was done for him at the end. When my mother and I were at the funeral, she told me that she had always figured that I might die by suicide, but she had never thought it was a possibility for him. I also had always thought about suicide for my own life, but now here was my brother. He had never discussed suicide with me, and it was a total surprise. I didn't blame him or question his reasons. I understood how he just could not continue to live. His pain was unholdable.

With my job, one of my responsibilities was to be on the suicide prevention work group at the medical school. We focused a lot on surveys and statistics. At the end of one of our meetings, I disclosed that it was the anniversary of my own brother's suicide. The conversation stopped being about facts and figures, and our group of psychiatrists and other medical providers began to relate to the personal human and emotional scope of our work.

I was appointed to the medical school's psychiatry faculty and helped train the young psychiatry residents. It seemed rather ironic to me that after being a patient of so many psychiatrists, here I was now in the role of helping train them. I would tell them the stories of my years of treatment for my own mental health conditions. I could tell that some of my stories—like the times of reparenting treatment and physical punishment—were shocking to them. I derived satisfaction from being able to teach them something they otherwise did not know. During these times, I was the expert, not the patient. I had never imagined that I would someday be in this role. I was always aware of an incredulity to it. Nevertheless, in the middle of my unexpected life, even with my work in suicide prevention, I struggled sometimes with my own feelings that I could not bear to remain in my life. I still confronted my own suicidal impulses.

Portland, 2020

The new year came—I had a feeling that the year 2020 was going to be an outstanding Red Letter Year. I never could have guessed that I was so wrong.

A new decade—but I barely survived the beginning. When I didn't show up at work on Friday to teach my peer mentoring class, my supervisor, Zoe, was concerned and came directly to my house to check on me. She found me undressed, unable to talk or even open the door for her. I could hardly even walk. The fire department came and broke down the back door, and I was taken by ambulance to the emergency department and later admitted to the Intensive Care Unit. I was diagnosed with a very rare and sometimes fatal disorder that was caused by the schizophrenia drugs I had taken for so many years—the same drugs that had saved my life and made it possible for me to heal and even be able to work. I was unconscious for the first days but finally awoke in the hospital and the doctor explained what had happened. Zoe had taken Ananda to her house and was taking care of her.

Suddenly, I could not take the schizophrenia drugs I depended on anymore. If I did, they could kill me.

After a week in the hospital I was allowed to return home. I wanted to go back to work as quickly as possible, even though my brain seemed to still need to heal. I saw more clearly how important it was for me to be connected to other people. I reached out to several people and became more connected to Kim, my next door neighbor, and a colleague named Laura.

And then the COVID-19 virus struck the world. The pandemic was upon us.

Instead of social connection, isolation became my daily

reality. In addition to this, without the schizophrenia drugs I had taken for so long, I began to sometimes experience hallucinations that had for so long been held at bay.

After the first ten days of social isolation became the governor's new requirement for Oregon, the Portland Police Bureau announced that emergency calls about attempted and threatened suicide had increased suddenly to an astounding degree. When I read this, I immediately realized I must do something to respond. As I worked from home because my office had been closed, I focused on designing and figuring out how to create a new program. It would be the type of program that I knew from my own firsthand experiences of being suicidal would help make a difference to people who were just hanging on to the edge. I had a vision for something new, something that I felt would be more effective than anything else that was available. Part of the vision was to use peer support specialists to provide contact to people who were struggling by giving daily support through text, phone, and video—in addition to the services provided by psychiatrists and counselors. It would mean a level of support and help that had not been possible for struggling people before, outside of an inpatient setting. I threw myself into this work with a sense of urgency.

Early one morning Billie called. She was weeping— could barely talk through the tears. In broken sentences she told me that Tim had taken an overdose and was dead. I tried to comfort her, but it was such an awful and fresh wound, there was not much I could say that could help. I tried to console her and let her know she was not alone, but the truth was because of the quarantine, she actually was very alone. With the requirements for social distancing due to the pandemic, she was isolated at a time when she really needed to be with other people. I wished I could just put my arms around her. But I couldn't. We made a plan to talk by phone every day.

The parts of my life that became the most essential were the daily walks with Ananda in the neighborhood and the daily check-in with Billie. On our walks it was always such a relief to see a neighbor and be able to even just say "hello" to another human.

Also, the gallery's show with work from so many artists from around the world was coming up soon—as soon as businesses would be allowed to reopen.

I had some more hallucinations, but even with them, I was able to be very productive with my professional work and my painting and writing. I started to work on a huge new canvas. It was a giant Winged Being, in different shades of blue, with gray and white wings.

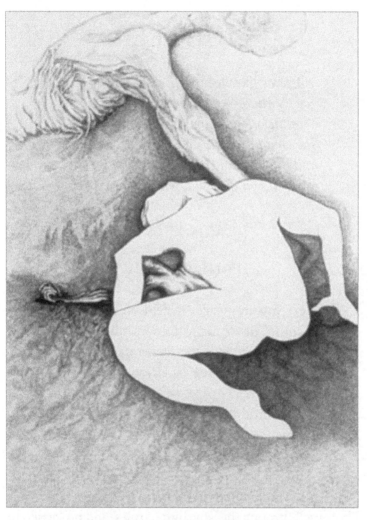

"Sickness, Old Age, and Death (No. 3)"
Pen and ink on paper
30 x 40 in.

EIGHTEEN

*And at that last minute, she saw poems
everywhere—in the trees, under the roots,
in the alley, on the fingers of monkeys—
she could hardly believe her ears and eyes—
and the last time I saw her, she was walking
down the road, whistling gayly.*

Portland, 2020

There was no peace—I held on to things the best I could, determined to continue, but every day was a huge struggle. Every day, was a question mark—could I do it? The isolation made things seem nearly impossible.

It was the middle of the night, and I simply could not go to sleep. I started having a very involved, detailed dream/fantasy. In my dream, I had purchased my ticket to Zurich—the plan was in place. I dreamed I contacted the Swiss organization that specializes in guiding the lost souls like myself through the labyrinth of rules, and processes, to the final goal of self-deliverance: medically assisted death. I would not exactly kill myself—they would do it for me. In my dream they were expecting me. I had rehearsed this in my mind many times—over and over. I dreamed it was all

Meghan J.M. Caughey

in place. Now that the actual time was here, at least in my imagination, it nearly felt automatic.

All that I needed to do was get on the plane and cruise at thirty-thousand feet in First Class to Zurich, where the experts in medically assisted death would shepherd me into oblivion. I was remarkably calm about it all. In my fantasy, the house had been closed up, and the donations of all my antique furniture, my clothes, and other meaningless possessions had been hauled away to the local charity where they would help people get back on their feet after being homeless—how could I not feel good about it?

I imagined that I was at the airport, at the gate. I had gone through security mechanically, noting how much easier it is when traveling without many possessions.

I had thought about saying goodbye to Luma, to Maggie, to Zoe, to Kent, and a few other people in my life, but no, it was best to just go, just disappear into the air. I imagined I had a few letters that I would mail to them once I got to Switzerland; I would time their delivery to happen after my final act, when it would be too late for them to stop me.

No regrets, no looking back.

No regrets.

Well, the part about "no regrets" wasn't completely true. My thoughts went to the time, years ago, when I had a gray striped cat named Finn, after an Irish war hero. Every night Finn would bring the dead animals he caught into the house and would leave them in the bedroom doorway where in the morning I would accidentally step on the carcasses. I was renting a room to a housemate, and Finn would often leave the bloody body parts of a mouse right outside her bedroom door. I couldn't tolerate it, and I wasn't so in love with him anyway. I guess I'm more of a Dog Person than a Cat Person. I told myself that I didn't care for him. One morning, after a particularly gruesome mouse carcass, I'd had enough. I put him in the cat carrier and took him back to the animal shelter where I had gotten him the season before. I gave him back: it was as simple as that. I didn't feel ruthless, I just felt like I could not awaken one more morning and step into the bloody mess of his night's hunted prey. I worried about my renter being upset, and I couldn't stand it any longer. I carried the cat carrier, with Finn inside, into the shelter, placed it on the desk and unemotionally told the woman that I couldn't keep him, so here he is, you take him. Then, I walked out the door, got into the station wagon, and drove home. Simple as that.

But it wasn't simple. I tried to convince myself it was better this way, that I had no real choice, that it didn't really matter anyway. I spent a day and a half trying not to think about it, trying to ignore my thoughts and feelings. It was for the better. I had done the only possible thing I could do. But I kept thinking about his little gray striped face, and the way he neatly tidied himself with his quick, pink tongue. I kept seeing his sweet, expressive fuzzy-striped tail. After a day and a half, I got back in the station wagon and drove to the animal shelter.

I went to the same woman at the desk and told her I had a change of heart and realized that I wanted him after all. The woman just blankly looked at me. After a very long pause, she finally softly said, "The kitty was put down this morning."

What?

No!

"It's too late," she said.

What had I done? I had killed him!

I remembered driving home; I could barely see the road through my tears.

So, this was the big regret of my life. I had killed my cat. There was no way to change it. I had to hold it in my awareness, acknowledge it, and feel compassion for the little cat, for the woman behind the desk, and finally, somehow, even for myself. And this was years ago anyway—why did it still loom so large in my mind—here in the middle of this endless, sleepless night?

In my imagination, I went through airport security, and then straight to the gate. I noticed a sign saying the flight was delayed. Four hours. It was OK; I wasn't in a hurry. At this point all I had was time. I found a seat by a large window. The sun had finally set. I stared out into the dark, watching the blue lights that marked the runways. I always loved the blue lights. They were like the best part of Christmas, without the bad parts. They demand nothing; instead they just glow quietly with soft reassurance, guiding the planes to safety.

I was peaceful about my decision to end my life; in fact it seemed natural—I had been rehearsing this conclusion for years. I stared in a daze out the window. I was just in this dreamy state when suddenly my phone awoke me by vibrating, signaling I had a message. I had meant to turn it off when I got into bed—how annoying. I automatically picked it up off the night table and glanced at the screen.

3:30 a.m.

It was a text message from Billie: "I can't do it anymore—sorry. forgive me."

I read it several times. What did it mean? I knew she had been having a hard time since Tim's death, but the last time we spoke she was more upbeat. She had reassured me she was OK. Had something happened? I reflexively called her. No answer.

I left a message: "Sweetheart, call me as soon as you get this."

I put the phone back on the table and stared into the dark, but now I was thinking about Billie. There was the nagging concern—was she OK? I picked the phone back up and stared at her message. I called her again. No answer.

"Billie, call me."

Damn. What was that girl doing? Now I was really starting to worry.

I decided I simply wouldn't worry about it. Forget about it. I couldn't worry about her. Not now. It was the middle of the night. I needed to sleep. But…what if something was wrong? I told myself to just let it go.

My phone vibrated. It was Billie.

"Billie, what's going on?"

"Oh Meghan, I'm so sorry. To bother you. It's just too—"

"Too what, Billie, where are you?"

"I'm at the Burnside Bridge. Don't be mad."

Damn that girl! Why in hell do I care about her? Burnside Bridge—it is known as a place where people jump to their sure death in the Willamette River below.

"Billie, what are you doing—are you OK?"

"I'm so sorry to bother you. I bother everyone."

"No, you don't. What are you doing?"

"It's Tim—I miss him too much. I have to go be with him."

I suddenly realized what she was saying. She was going to end it all.

"Billie, wait, talk to me! Come on now!"

"It's no use. I just can't do it anymore."

"Wait—talk to me! Will you just hold on?"

She was crying, I could hear it. Fear flooded through me.

"Billie, wait—I'm coming to the bridge. Wait for me!"

"I can't! I just can't—can't anymore!"

"Billie, you've got to! I'll be there as soon as I can. Half hour. Stay right there!"

"I don't know, Meghan—I don't—"

"I'll be there as soon as I can. Just wait. Billie—I'm counting on you!"

"I'll try, but I don't know."

"You wait for me! I'm coming now!"

"I'll try!" And then she hung up.

As quickly as I could, I threw on some clothes and ran and got into my car. Everything was taking way too long, moving in slow-motion through the dark, empty streets.

Please, Billie, I prayed to myself.

Finally, after what seemed like hours, I made it to the bridge. I saw Billie standing by the railing along the edge, looking very small, her face tear wet from tears. I leapt out of the car. She saw me and suddenly our eyes connected.

"Meghan, I just don't see how I can go on," she stuttered.

"I know, Sweetheart! Sometimes you just have to go on, anyway. You just have to."

I put my arms around her, and she collapsed into me. I swooped her up. She sobbed, and I held her.

"I know you hurt bad, Sweetie, but I promise you its gonna get better. You just gotta hold on." In the back of my mind I had the thought of how impossible it was to be telling her to go on, when I wasn't always sure I could do it myself. Then I realized that I would simply have to live—I couldn't let her down.

For years I had confidently said to people who were looking to me for hope that "I have gone through the fire and come out the other side, and so can you."

But now, I had to stop and question this—was it really true?

Suddenly, I had a new realization: One can go into the fire—and just be there—in the middle of the flames—and survive. Sometimes, the point isn't to go in, and then come out. Sometimes we must just be willing to go be in the middle of the intense heat, among the flames, and instead of counting on getting out the other side, just be right there, in the middle of it. We don't always know if there will be another side beyond the flames. This spot, in the middle of it all, is where true courage is practiced. We stay in the flames and allow everything extraneous in ourselves to be burned away. We just stay.

We are left with ourselves, nothing more, or less. And it is enough.

I wasn't willing to let her down. And I wasn't willing to let anyone else down. I am alive. It is up to me to use this life of mine. Is this love? I'm not completely sure, but I know that this is more important than anything else I can do. I will work out the life thing—make it up as I go along. Maybe I can use the images in my drawings and paintings to help communicate with people. I will write poems. I will find ways to connect. This is the most important thing. This is my reason to live. This is my sacred purpose. I held on to Billie as she trembled and cried.

I don't know how I am going to do it, but I will find a way.

I don't know what comes next.

I'm in the middle of the fire.

I am here.

"Human Being, Female (No. 4)"
Pen and ink
Detail